PROGRESS

—— VS ——

PARASITES

DOUGLAS CARSWELL grew up in Uganda.
Elected to Parliament four times, for
two different parties, he ended up as an
independent MP. Douglas co-founded Vote
Leave, the official campaign that won the
referendum to take the United Kingdom out
of the European Union. He stood down from
Parliament in 2017, having accomplished
what he went into politics to achieve.

DOUGLAS CARSWELL

PROGRESS

——— VS ———

PARASITES

A BRIEF HISTORY OF THE CONFLICT THAT'S SHAPED OUR WORLD

HEAD
of ZEUS

An Apollo Book

This is an Apollo book, a substantially revised and updated edition
of *Rebel*, first published in the UK in 2017 by Head of Zeus Ltd
This paperback edition published by Head of Zeus Ltd in 2019

9 7 5 3 1 2 4 6 8

A catalogue record for this book is available from
the British Library.

ISBN (PBO): 9781786691569
ISBN (E): 9781789542783

Typeset by Adrian McLaughlin

Printed and bound in Great Britain by
CPI Group (UK) Ltd, Croydon CR0 4YY

Head of Zeus Ltd
First Floor East
5–8 Hardwick Street
London EC1R 4RG

WWW.HEADOFZEUS.COM

To Clementine and Kitty

CONTENTS

CONTENTS

INTRODUCTION

FROM FLINT STONES
TO SMARTPHONES

Digging for potatoes in my vegetable patch one summer's evening a few years ago, I came across a weird-looking stone. Sharply pointed at one end, its rounded base fitted neatly into the palm of my hand. It felt almost as if it had been made to be held. As I washed the mud off in the kitchen sink, I realized what it was; I was holding a Stone-Age hand axe.

If it was as ancient as some of the flint tools once found on the other side of the valley, it could have been produced by Homo heidelbergensis, an early type of human being, perhaps a quarter of a million years ago.

Then a series of thoughts struck me: An actual individual had made this. What were they like? I might be the first person to have held their handiwork since they dropped it here all that time ago. What sort of life did he or she have in this place we now call Essex in England? Were they happy in those few fleeting years before they, like their hand axe, were returned to the soil?

Mulling all that over, I then went and did something very twenty-first-century. I took out my iPhone, and with the hand axe in one hand, took a photo of it with the other; two hand-held tools, each the cutting-edge technology of their day, held a few inches apart, yet separated by many thousands of years of human progress.

One, the hand axe, made from a single material, flint, was almost certainly the work of a single person, too. It is pretty primitive, even by Stone-Age standards, with a crude style that the archaeologists who study these things call 'Clactonian' – named after the town of Clacton in England where these types of stone tools were first uncovered. Appropriately enough, my vegetable patch sits only a few miles from the town.

Clactonian hand axes have none of the sophistication of later stone tools, such as the Acheulean or the Levallois hand axes. They are not made by carving something, chip by chip, out of a larger block. Instead, a lump of flint has been hammered with another stone around the edges to give it a shape that can be used to cut and scrape. All that bashing probably happened right where my house and garden now stand, or at least within a few miles or so.

Contrast that to the way my iPhone has been made. It's packed with multiple materials. About 40 per cent of the weight of an iPhone consists of iron and aluminium, but there's also copper, cobalt, chromium and nickel in there, too. About 6 per cent is silicon. There are minuscule amounts of more complex compounds, such as yttrium, neodymium, europium, gadolinium and, not to forget, terbium.

Multiple different materials go into producing any one of an iPhone's component parts: a gleaming screen, behind which sit neat rows of microchips pressed onto printed boards; a battery, from which flows the electric current that brings it all to life.

Imagine the extraordinary complexity that must go into producing any one of those parts. The sleek plastic casing alone is the product of an extraordinarily complex process of extracting oil, then distilling it, before transporting it across distant oceans. At each stage, thousands of people have contributed to the web of processes that produced the smartphone in your pocket.

The story of human progress is about how we moved from a world of simple self-sufficiency, where we could not create much more than sharpened stones, to today's world of complex interdependence, providing us with all that we have around us. How did we get from one to the other?

'It's just a case of being cleverer,' you might think.

'We have more sophisticated technology than our primitive ancestors because we have bigger brains.'

It's easy to assume that because we live in a world of greater technological sophistication, we must therefore be brainier than those who lived before us. Actually, if you compare the brain sizes of modern humans to archaic Homo sapiens, or Neanderthals, it's clear that if anything they – not us – had bigger individual brains, although we should not assume this meant they were cleverer in a cognitive sense. Since we went from having hand axes to having smartphones, it's not our individual brains that have got better in any sense, but what the author Matt Ridley calls our collective brain.

What do I mean by a collective brain?

You don't need to know much to make a hand axe. Even the uninitiated could work out for themselves how to hammer out something similar, rock against rock, in a few hours. But to produce something as sophisticated as a smartphone, you need to work with others.

There is no one person who knows enough to make a smartphone from scratch, not even the late Steve Jobs. When the Apple team designed the first smartphone, they incorporated into their design chips that others had engineered and screen technology that third-parties had perfected. Each of the individual parts that make up a smartphone is itself a product of countless actions, undertaken by tens of thousands of individuals, among whom none contributes more than a tiny input of the overall knowledge needed.

Apple might manage the supply chain that assembles the various component parts but beyond that there is no central direction. The people who mined the cobalt knew nothing of those who designed the software, who were oblivious of the company that created the chips. Yet together that vast sum of know-how produces a collective intelligence capable of producing something of far greater sophistication than that which, as individuals, we would ever be capable of. How did this come about?

'Somewhere in Africa more than 100,000 years ago,' Matt Ridley suggests, humankind 'began to add to its habits, generation by generation.'* We learnt that instead of self-sufficiency, we could draw on the knowledge and efforts of others. Humans, uniquely, started to specialize in producing what they produced well, and then to exchange what it was they produced for what others had specialized in producing.

This change was barely perceptible at first. There are only a few clues in the archaeological record – sea shells or ochre exchanged over long distances – that hint at a nascent exchange. Yet from such humble beginnings, an evermore sophisticated process of specialization and

* See Ridley, M., *The Rational Optimist: How Prosperity Evolves* (2010).

exchange has, over time and often very slowly, lifted our species from a subsistence existence to a world of cities and shopping centres. Working together through exchange is what sets our species apart. It is what enables us today to order what we want online, eat fresh salad in mid-winter, or cross the Atlantic at 30,000 feet.

To appreciate the extent to which interdependence has elevated us from hand axes to smartphones, try this little thought experiment: imagine that you had to try to produce many of the things you take for granted around you from scratch.

Forget about being self-sufficient at making a smartphone. Start with something more basic, like the house you live in. Would you be able to build it yourself, not only brick by brick, but by physically making each brick in the first place? And what about each door frame and pane of glass?

Or try something a little smaller, like the clothes that you wear. Assuming you found a way of producing enough wool to knit your own garments, your dress sense might start to look a little homemade.

How about something even more basic, such as producing a loaf of bread? I don't just mean could you bake bread in the oven. Would you be able to grow the wheat, mill it, and then find somewhere to extract salt from the sea? If my family had had to rely on my efforts in the vegetable patch to feed us, we would have all starved long ago. Instead most of us are able to buy the food, clothes and housing that we need by depending on the efforts of others.

Just as we depend on others specializing in the complex processes that produce what we need, we, too, specialize in something – it's called having a job. Whether we work as a brain surgeon or an Uber driver, we in effect swap what we do for things produced by the efforts of others.

You might imagine that the journey from hand axes to smartphones was slow but steady. Progress was certainly slow for most of human history, but it has been anything but even. For most of the millennia that separate these two objects, there was very little progress at all. Almost all human progress has happened over the past few thousand years, if not the past couple of centuries. For most people on the planet, things only really accelerated in the past few decades.

Most people who have lived since my hand axe was made would not have noticed any discernible improvement in technology during the course of their lives. Almost identical Clactonian hand axes continued to be made for tens of thousands of years, only slowly giving way to the slightly superior Acheulean designs. These evolved slowly into the slightly more sophisticated Levallois design – but the process took many millennia.

It wasn't until sixty thousand years ago that bows and arrows first appeared. It took another ten thousand years before the needle was invented, followed by the fish hook about twenty thousand years ago.

Eventually the Paleolithic – literally the 'old stone' age – gave way to the Neolithic – 'new stone' age. After that, some people discovered that they could get food by sowing crops, rather than gathering them. Farming began. Stone tools eventually gave way to ones made from bronze and then iron.

Yet even once things started to accelerate about ten thousand years ago, if you pick almost any period in it, those alive would have been using pretty much the same types of tools to perform the same sort of tasks as their great, great, great, great, great grandparents had done before them. It's only really in the past few centuries that innovation and invention have happened at a speed such that one might notice their impact over the span of a single human life. It's only in the past few decades that most of the components that go into an iPhone have been made possible.

Technology is, of course, only one measure of progress. Even slower to get going than technological progress was any improvement in living standards. Grinding poverty has been the default condition of our species for most of our existence.

Angus Maddison, the economic historian, has calculated output per person globally over the past three thousand years, and shows that until about three hundred years

WORLD GDP PER CAPITA OVER THE LAST TWO MILLENNIA

Total output of the world economy; adjusted for inflation
and expressed in 2011 international dollars.

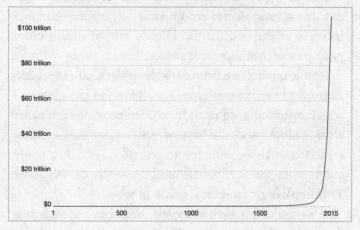

GDP, or Gross Domestic Product, per person is the value of all
goods and services produced by a country in one year divided by
the country's population. Maddison calculated the GDP per person
in 1990 US dollar prices. Source: World GDP – Our World In Data
based on World Bank & Maddison (2017)

ago people had a subsistence existence, hunger never far
away.*

So why didn't we get richer as our technology got gradually better? Incremental improvements in technology
over the past ten thousand years – better types of metal

---

* See Maddison, A., *Contours of the World Economy 1–2030 AD:
Essays in Macro-Economic History* (2007).

tool, improved crop varieties, irrigation, advances in milling – might have enabled people to produce more food. But until a few generations ago, that increase in output was almost always accompanied by a corresponding increase in the population. Higher output meant more poor people, not more per person.*

People might have been capable of the kind of specialization and exchange that we see all around us today, and which eventually led us to be able to provide each other with iPhones and the rest of our twenty-first-century standard of living. But for some reason it didn't really seem to happen at any scale until very recently. Why not? This book is an attempt to explain why.

For most of human history, specialization and exchange has been inhibited by small elites, who rigged society for their own advantage. With the productive unable to escape the parasitic, per-capita output in most societies remained low.

There were, however, a few fleeting exceptions to this. Hidden within Maddison's aggregate global data, there was a sustained increase in output per person in the republics of Greece and Rome, over the course of a few generations. Then in the Middle Ages, we can see some evidence of an increase in output per person

---

* See Clark, G., *A Farewell to Alms: A Brief Economic History of the World* (2007).

on a small scale in Venice, and perhaps too on a larger scale in Abbasid Iraq and Song China. We know, also, that something rather striking happened in the Dutch Republic at the start of the early modern era.

Whenever there was a sustained interest in per-capita output, specialization and exchange had been allowed to happen. Power in these societies was dispersed. The elites that might otherwise inhibit the productive were themselves inhibited. The Greeks were a diffuse collection of city-states, some run as democracies or oligarchies, not just monarchies. Rome constrained the powerful by replacing kings with competing consuls and magistrates. The Venetians and then the Dutch dispersed power with complex – some might say chaotic – constitutions.

Those at the apex of such societies were less able to interfere with every aspect of social and economic life. Trade and exchange could be conducted on the terms set by the buyer and the seller, not any overlord. Accumulating wealth ceased to be synonymous with holding power. It was possible to earn a living without needing someone else's permission.

Laws in such societies could be codified, becoming more than just a statement of what the powerful wanted at any one time. Property rights were relatively secure. Systems of what we would today call corporate governance emerged to allow those with capital to take risks with it, knowing that their liabilities were limited.

But as we shall also see, until around AD 1800, when these kinds of conditions arose in a society, they tended not to last very long. In Greece, Rome and Venice the parasitic eventually overwhelmed the productive. Early signs of take-off in China and elsewhere stalled. Per-capita output fell back again.

Since 1800, we have seen a prolonged period of increases in output per person. It's not perhaps the duration of this period of progress that is so striking – Rome and Venice had a couple of centuries of rising output per person, too; it's the sheer scale of it that is different.

Beginning in north-western Europe and America, then spreading to Japan and east Asia, south America, India and now Africa, a succession of societies has emerged in which the productive have been (relatively) free to exchange without extortion from the parasitic. The phenomenon is not limited to a few exceptional states in the Mediterranean anymore. It seems to have gone global.

Why is it that power ends up being dispersed in some societies, but not others? Why are the inhibitors inhibited in some places, but allowed free rein to extort in others? And why have those conditions that allow the productive to escape the parasitic gone from being exceptional to ubiquitous?

'It's all about institutions,' is the commonplace explanation. Powerful elites are able to extort where there are 'extractive' institutions, such as powerful kingships or bodies controlled by rapacious nobles.

Where, on the other hand, these institutionalists explain, there are institutions that happened to be more 'inclusive' – a Senate and elected magistrates in Rome, or a Great Council in Venice, or an English Parliament – the elites could not have everything their own way. The productive interest had some protection.

The existence of extractive institutions certainly helps explain how elites have been able to extort from the productive. It does not do enough to tell us why.

Nor is it simple chance that explains the shape of a society's institutions. The shape of a society's institutions reflect the underlying attitudes and insights within that society. It is these that ultimately explain if freedom is able to flourish in a certain society.

To understand why the default human condition has been poverty, it's important to begin by appreciating that the default human belief system has been in some form of divine design. Since prehistoric times people believed that they, and the world around them, were shaped by supernatural agency. Our ancestors seem to have projected intentions onto natural events, be it a thunder storm or an outbreak of disease.

This tendency to assume deliberate agency lies behind everything has had important implications. It has prevented us from appreciating the extent to which order emerges spontaneously, without any extraneous agency at all.

If people believe the world is ordered from on high, they are half way to accepting that there should be orders from on high. Accepting divine design in celestial affairs can morph into an expectation of deliberate design in human ones. If there is a celestial plan, then those mandated with heavenly authority become planners. It is not a coincidence that extractive elites, who have been with us since before the pyramids were built, often sit at the apex of society with a religious role as pharaohs or priests, as well as princes.

For freedom to flourish, it needs to be recognized that the world around us is self-ordering. Once we see that everything from the stars to the seasons, to the evolution of our species is part of a self-arranging system, we cease to see ourselves as mere extras in some heavenly play. It is this that opens up the possibility that we might arrange things for ourselves with our own agency, free from any overlords. It is far harder to insist on organising human affairs from on high when the world is regarded as self-arranging.

'But surely,' you might wonder, 'if ideas about self-order help explain why the productive in some societies were able to free themselves from the parasitic, we might expect to see such ideas flourishing in places where per-capita output increased?' That is exactly what did happen.

Insights about the self-ordering nature of the world permeated certain schools of thought in ancient Greece and Rome, and the inhibitors were inhibited. For a brief interlude, it was understood by many that agency was a question of human action, not the whim of gods. Ideas about human nature and nature itself, which might seem to our minds to be strikingly modern, existed in antiquity until they were extinguished with the coming of new versions of monotheistic creeds. A millennium of Malthusian misery ensued.

Slowly, however, insights about self-order arose again, nagging away at the established orthodoxies which insisted on there being deliberate design. Yet each time someone taught that the world was in some way self-ordering, from Jan Hus in matters of religion, Giordano Bruno on the nature of the cosmos, Adam Smith on the nature of morality, or Charles Darwin on the natural world itself, they were opposed by those to whom such notions were not merely an affront, but a threat. No matter how pious the priests Hus and Bruno were, they were accused of atheism, the most obvious charge laid against anyone that advocates self-order.

From the eighteenth century onwards, during the Enlightenment, it became far harder to suppress ideas about self-order. Unlike Hus or Bruno, neither Smith nor Darwin were burnt at the stake for their heretical thoughts.

It's hardly controversial to point out that the Enlightenment, a revolution in the way people thought, preceded the start of the exponential increase in global output per person that came afterwards. Scientific method and reason began to replace custom and tradition as a source of authority in the minds of many men and women, undermining the old order across much of Europe and, in time, beyond. But it would be a mistake to then suggest that the Enlightenment is simply synonymous with human progress.

Far from eradicating the age old insistence that human society be arranged from above by deliberate design, the Enlightenment gave such demands a new – at times murderous – lease of life. Small elites invoked reason, and the dangerous illusion of absolute truth, to order the affairs of millions. Instead of setting people free, the Enlightenment spawned a series of secular creeds – Jacobinism, communism, fascism and socialism – which bound them as tightly as any of the older orthodoxies. Each of these secular religions brought with them a priesthood of planners, certain of their own authority and ability to achieve an earthly perfection. More often it was hell.

Far from achieving human progress, these Enlightenment creeds inhibited human progress in all kinds of ways. Far from facilitating specialization and exchange, those that tried to direct society by design remained hostile to any notion of spontaneous economic order. In the name of reason, human progress has been repeatedly hindered and halted – and at times, savagely reversed.

What enables freedom to flourish is not a blueprint, but the realization that the world is self-ordering and does not need a blueprint. It's the acceptance that none of us has the knowledge we need to produce a single iPhone – nor scarcely even a loaf of bread from scratch. So, what makes anyone so certain that they know all they need to know to be able to arrange a whole society?

Alas, even today this point is not appreciated. Quite the contrary, in fact. There is an entrenched insistence that human social and economic affairs can best be arranged by top-down design.

In many Western states, a technocratic elite has emerged, presuming – like latter-day Jacobins – to know how to order society to produce certain outcomes. Governments believe they know better than their citizens how they might spend their money. Central bankers, apparently, know how to engineer prosperity. Bureaucratic programmes are presumed to be able to alleviate social problems.

As so often happens when a small elite is intent on ordering the affairs of others by design, spontaneous economic order comes under attack. Supranational officials increasingly regulate and control free exchanges. On campuses across Europe and America, students are taught that trade, far from being the engine of our elevation, is somehow inherently exploitative.

If you believe that progress does not just happen but requires intervention, the notion that there could have been progress before – without your blueprint – can start to seem offensive. Those intent on organizing society by blueprint are almost always ambivalent about the idea that there has been human progress in the first place.

Many of the political Left in Britain, Europe and America ignore the irrefutable improvement in the human condition that has happened over the past few centuries. The story of increases in output per person is scripted as a tale of environmental degradation and colonial exploitation. There have even been some recent bestselling books that suggest humankind is not really any better off now than we were in the Paleolithic past, when we lived a life of pristine simplicity in some kind of Arcadia, apparently.

Rather than marvel at the fact that tens of millions of people around the planet today live longer, healthier lives than they did a generation ago, we are invited to believe that material progress has somehow atomized us as individuals, leaving us miserable and lonely. Far from celebrating the elevation of the human condition, we are invited to adopt an almost pre-modern belief that humanity sits once more on the brink of some sort of catastrophe – from which only the priesthood of techno-crats, and economic redistribution, can save us.

Salvation, today's parasites suggest, as they have in

every age, can only come from sacrificing our wealth and freedom to others. This book shows why calls for economic redistribution are not just wrong, but that they are today what they have always been – a persistent pretext for parasitism.

To ensure human progress continues, we need to keep sight of the simple insight about the self-ordering nature of the world around us. It is *that*, not any grand plan, that underpins all human progress. This book sets out a series of radical changes, shaped by insights about self-order, needed to not just safeguard specialization and exchange, but ensure it increases exponentially.

When we see a hand axe today, we look at something that has become utterly obsolete. Mine now serves as a paperweight in a study that hardly even uses much paper anymore. If specialization and exchange are free to carry on – shaping and reshaping, innovating and inventing – then one day soon we might look at smartphones in much the same way. By then, the way we currently earn a living might seem almost as archaic as hunting and gathering.

PART I

THE PRODUCTIVE
AND THE PARASITIC

1

THE BEST OF TIMES

Terror attacks. Migration crises. Wars in the Middle East. Oceans turned to acid and polluted by plastic. Catastrophic changes to the climate. Gender inequality and social injustice.

You don't have to look very far to find evidence that the world is getting worse. We seem to be bombarded by bad news. Television is packed with pessimism. Newspapers report with relish about all kinds of calamity. Our Twitter timelines swarm with indignation about the latest outrage.

In recent decades, we have been warned about all kinds of impending disasters. In the 1970s, oil was apparently going to run out and a new Ice Age was on the way. Then in the 1980s, it was acid rain and nuclear war that were supposed to wipe us out. After that came warnings

3

of overpopulation and epidemics, famine and rising sea levels. Today it's global warming that's going to get us, if an asteroid impact doesn't find us first.

But despite all these doom scenarios, the world hasn't actually got worse. In fact, it's been getting better. For most people there has never been a more comfortable time to be alive than right now.

That's not to say that there aren't all sorts of instances of individual suffering – for refugees in Burma or Syria, or indeed for plenty of people from London to Los Angeles. But for most of us, in most countries on the planet, life is better today by almost every conceivable measure of well-being than it has ever been before.

BETTER LIFE

For a start, there's a lot more human life on the planet now than there ever has been.

There are an estimated 7.5 billion of us alive right now – twice as many as in 1965. Which in turn was double the number living a century before that; and which in turn was also about twice as many people as existed in the mid-seventeenth century.

'But,' you might interject, 'doesn't more people just make everything more crowded and polluted? Don't all those extra people mean less for everyone else?'

There are not just more people on the planet, but we are better fed and clothed, living in better housing and cleaner cities, than ever before.

Worldwide, a baby is half as likely to die today as one born in 1990. Infant mortality is down almost 90 per cent in the UK since 1960. The most dramatic improvement has happened in Asia, where infant mortality is now lower than it was in the UK in the 1960s. Back then, out of every 1,000 babies born worldwide, 113 died before their first birthday. Today, that number is down to 32.

We are living longer. Life expectancy in America in 1950 was sixty-eight years. Today, it is seventy-nine. In Britain since 1980, life expectancy has extended each year by an average of thirteen weeks for men and nine weeks for women. Anyone in Britain who makes it to the age of 100 gets a special birthday message from the Queen. When Elizabeth II first ascended to the throne in 1952, she sent a few dozen personalized telegrams to the country's centenarians each year. Almost seventy years later, she sends out almost eight thousand such messages a year – so many, in fact, that the palace has had to instigate a slightly more automated process for sending out her good wishes so that she doesn't find herself having to sign dozens of such messages a day.

In 1960, average life expectancy worldwide was fifty-two years. Today it's seventy-one. On average, that means over a third more life for everyone. In many countries, like Mexico, where life expectancy was once way below the Western average, it has now more or less drawn level, at seventy-five years.

African life expectancy is up almost eight years over the past four decades. In Uganda, where I grew up in the 1970s and 80s, life expectancy was forty-something – and falling. Today it's sixty-something – and rising so fast it'll soon draw level with Europe and America. Many of the big killer diseases are being defeated. Deaths from malaria are down from 166,000 in 2009 to below 100,000 in 2018. There are now almost no deaths from malaria outside of Africa. Rates of HIV infection, once frighteningly high in Sub-Saharan Africa, have dropped dramatically, too. Thanks to advances in science, retroviral treatments are available that mean that this once incurable disease is now a manageable condition. Falling rates of infection and better medicine help explain why the number of people dying of AIDS each year fell from 1.5 million in 2003 to 800,000 by 2014.

Stroke deaths in the US have halved since 1990. In South Korea, they have fallen by about two-thirds. UK road traffic deaths have fallen from almost eight thousand in 1965 to less than two thousand today – and that is with many times more cars on the roads. Heart disease in the United States fell by half between 1963 and 1990, and it has almost halved again since. Cancer survival rates are also increasing. In 1975, cancer killed 187 per 100,000 UK men. Today, that number is down to 125. In the US, deaths from cancer are down by a fifth since the 1970s. The type of skin cancer that killed my big sister, Alice, in the prime of her life almost two decades ago is no longer incurable.

RICHER

We are not only living longer, but are, on average, much better off than before as well. In Britain, we are more than twice as rich as our grandparents, and a third better off than we were even thirty years ago. The average income in the UK today is 119 per cent* higher than in 1950, and 29 per cent† up on what it was in 1990. In America, average incomes have risen over that period by 130 per cent‡ and 35 per cent§ respectively. The rise

---

* Figures derived from the *Annual Abstract of Statistics 1950*, which shows the Average Gross Weekly Earnings (AGWE) for adult male and female manual workers. Uses the same PPP exchange as USD for conversion as the OECD source.

† OECD Average Annual Wages, using the 2015 constant prices at 2015 USD PPPs (https://stats.oecd.org/Index.aspx?DataSetCode= AV_AN_WAGE#).

‡ Average Wage Indexing Series of the Social Security Administration. Figure from 1951.

§ OECD Average Annual Wages, using the 2015 constant prices at 2015 USD PPPs (https://stats.oecd.org/Index.aspx?DataSetCode= AV_AN_WAGE#).

in incomes has been even more dramatic in countries like Spain, where incomes have risen four-fold since 1960, and the Netherlands, up almost three-fold since 1960. The average Japanese income today is almost five times what it was in 1960 – and that's despite two decades of lost economic growth.*

To be sure, there are still some pockets of deprivation even in rich Western countries. But even the poorest households in America and Britain today enjoy household goods and a standard of living that half a century ago would have been the preserve of the rich.

As a schoolboy recently arrived in the UK in the mid-1980s, I listened to a succession of geography and economics teachers drone on about Britain's apparent industrial decline. Yet, post-industrial Britain is a myth. Manufacturing output has not fallen – it's higher today than ever before. 'De-industrialized' Britain, for example, makes more cars than ever before.

All that has happened is that others make even more than we do – and when we produce what we do, we do so without the need to employ millions of labourers in factories on minimal wages. Output is up, despite the fact that a mere 8 per cent of jobs are in manufacturing – compared to one in four in the late 1970s.

Nor has America de-industrialized. US industrial out-

* See TradingEconomics.com for details.

put right now is twice what it was in 1980, and it's almost three times what it was when Lyndon Johnson was in the White House.*

So-called 'de-industrialization' is not a loss of industry but rather a reduction in the number of people it takes to produce an ever-greater amount of goods. We make more per worker, which means we don't need as many people to toil for as long.

In 1913, the average American worker clocked up 1,036 hours a year – compared to a mere 746 hours in 2003. (For Brits, it was 1,181 hours worked in 1913 and 694 in 2003.) Despite only putting in about half the hours, workers got paid far more. In 1913, average pay in the US was US$5.12 per hour. By 2003, it was almost eight times that amount: US$38.92 per hour (both at 1990 prices).

Among those officially classified as 'poor' in America, 99 per cent live in homes that have electricity, water and a fridge; 95 per cent have a television; 88 per cent have a phone; 71 per cent own a car; 70 per cent have air conditioning. In 1950, many middle-class Americans did not have many of those things.

In 1969, only rich people had television sets, since they cost the equivalent of a month's wages. Today, they cost less than two days' wages. In 1951, just 14 per cent of

* See HumanProgress.org data on US manufacturing output.

UK households had a car. Now 6 per cent of households own four. Most homes in the UK did not have central heating in 1970. Now almost all of them do.

'People in rich countries might have grown richer,' I hear you thinking. 'But what about those in poorer countries?' Actually, the poorer countries have been growing rich even faster. So much so that countries we once rather condescendingly called 'Third World' have been developing at a much faster pace than the so-called 'First World'.

With a handful of exceptions, like Afghanistan, Syria and Somalia, almost every country today is better off than it was in the mid-twentieth century. The standout example of progress over the past few decades is China.

In 1950, the average person living in China was not simply poor. They were poorer than their ancestors would have been two thousand years before. The average per person output in China in 1950, according to Angus Maddison's calculations looking at estimated output per person, was little different from what it had been in AD 50!

Yet since 1950, GDP per capita in China has increased by almost 9,000 per cent. The country – home to a fifth of humankind – has gone from rice paddies to iPads in two generations. In the past decade alone, Chinese GDP per capita has risen five-fold – a larger leap in ten years than China experienced at any time between the birth of

Jesus and the death of Mao. In 1981, almost nine in ten Chinese were living in extreme poverty. Now it's fewer than one in ten.

In the early 1980s, one in three Chinese was illiterate. Today, adult literacy is as close as it's possible to get to 100 per cent.

Since 1990, the number of people in China living on US$1.90 a day (in today's prices) has fallen from 670 million to about 20 million – perhaps the largest single reduction in poverty in human history. China is now home to more billionaires than America. A country that was unable to feed itself in the 1960s, today spawns tech giants like Ali Baba and Baidu. Expenditure on health care has risen five-fold in just twenty-five years. Chinese scientists pioneer gene therapy and clone technology.

It's not just China. In 1980, GDP per capita in India was US$271. Today it's over US$1,500. Worldwide, average incomes rose by 57 per cent between 1980 and 2015. Average income in Africa rose by 68 per cent. The average person living in Botswana today has a higher standard of living than the average Finn had in 1955.*

In fact, the whole world is on average much better off than before. In the mid-1960s the average income per person on the planet was US$6,000 a year. Today it's

* Ridley, M., *The Rational Optimist: How Prosperity Evolves* (2010), p. 15.

US$16,000. Of course, not everyone is better off. But in 1981, just half the world had access to clean water. Today, 91 per cent does. Over the past twenty-five years, an additional quarter of a million people have gained access to safe drinking water every day!

Worldwide, almost everyone eats better today than they did in the mid-1960s. Average calorie intake is up from 2,300 per person to 2,800. That's almost a fifth more food, making overconsumption, rather than hunger, a bigger public policy problem in many countries.

Since 1990, the proportion of human beings suffering from malnutrition has fallen from 19 per cent to 11 per cent. Thanks to new strains of wheat, produce is up seven times what it was in 1965 in India and Pakistan. In that same year, 43 per cent of people in developing countries lived in extreme poverty, defined as an income of US$1 or less at 1990 prices. Today, that proportion has fallen to 21 per cent. For the first time in human history, the share of the world's population living in extreme poverty – defined as less than US$1.90 per day – is now less than 10 per cent, and falling rapidly. The global price of food has fallen by 22 per cent since 1960. Workers worldwide have 17 per cent more free time than they did in 1950. Child labour has halved since 1990.

Each year, tens of millions of new middle-class Indians, Chinese, Turks and South Americans join the global economy. They live middle-class lifestyles, reflected by a surge in demand for everything from cars to fridges, air conditioning to air travel – and university places. As the world has become more prosperous, more children have been sent to school for longer. In 1950, the average African had one year of education, compared to six today. Britons had an average of six years of schooling in 1950. That has since doubled to twelve. Globally, the average child can expect eight years of education. Critically, from a developmental perspective, in many countries girls can access education as easily as boys.

We are not only better off, but we all benefit from technologies that allow us to do things that once only rich people could do. It's not just that fewer people had a TV – there was less to watch. In England in the 1980s, there were only four channels. Today we have a wide array to choose from, plus on-demand streaming that lets you watch what you want, when you want.

In the 1970s, air travel was so expensive that people who flew regularly were referred to as the Jet Set. Today, the cost of air tickets is so cheap that tens of millions can fly. So many millions of middle-class Chinese can now afford to fly that China is having to build the equivalent of a dozen new Heathrow or JFK airports each year just to cope.

In the 1970s, international phone calls were so expensive that Brits with relatives in Australia would save up to call them at Christmas. Calls were so difficult, you had to book ahead to make one via a telephone operator. Today, my nine-year-old is free to chat away to her cousin in Melbourne using a tablet on Sunday mornings.

Oh, and as if that was not good enough, we are – for the most part – a lot safer than before too. In the United States, the murder rate has dropped dramatically since the mid-1990s. Cumulatively, there are 600,000 more Americans alive today who would not have been had the US homicide rate in 1995 remained constant.*

In Britain, violent crime – despite recent headlines – has fallen dramatically too, down from 4.2 million recorded violent crimes in England and Wales in 1994–95 to 1.3 million recorded in 2016–17.† Globally, the UN tells us that the number of people dying violently has fallen by 6 per cent since the year 2000.

Of course, there are still savage conflicts. Terror attacks in France, Iraq, Afghanistan and West Africa have killed thousands. Tens of thousands of Syrians have perished

---

* The fall in US homicide rates is partly attributable to improvements in the medical treatment of victims of shootings and stabbings. More people are surviving such attacks. But there has also been a dramatic fall in the number of shootings and stabbings in America in the first place.

† According to the Crime Survey for England and Wales 2015, violent crime peaked in 1995. Despite some evidence of recent increases in violent crime since 2014, the overall trend over the past decade has been down.

in the conflict there, with millions more displaced. UN statistics are of little consolation to someone who has had to try to live through the catastrophes that have unfolded in Syria, Sudan, Iraq and Rwanda over the past few decades. But even taking all of that into account, as a person living on the planet today, you have less chance of coming to a grisly end at the hand of another human than at any point in history.

GREENER

And did I mention that the world has become cleaner and greener, too? There were 99 per cent fewer oil spills last year than there were in 1970. A moving car in 2017 emits less pollution than a stationary car did in 1970. China has taken the Giant Panda off the endangered list. British rivers and waterways are cleaner now than they have been for two hundred years. Having been hunted to extinction, beavers are back living in rivers in England after an absence of almost a thousand years. Global CFC emissions have been dramatically cut; so much so that the hole in the ozone is disappearing. The earth is literally getting greener thanks to a naturally-occurring process known as global greening. There has been a large, gradual increase in green vegetation on our planet since the 1970s.

Thirty years ago, the US produced 20 million tons of sulphur dioxide a year, and emitted 34 million tons of particulates. Today? Sulphur dioxide emissions are down to 4 million tons a year, and the amount of particulates has fallen by over a third.

Ranga Myneni, a scientist at Boston University, has used satellite photos to show that the amount of green vegetation cover on earth is up 14 per cent over the past thirty years – in almost all ecological systems. As Zaichun Zhu of Beijing University puts it, this is equivalent to adding a new green continent twice the size of mainland USA over the course of one lifetime. Global greening, rather than global warming, is surely the really big environmental news of our time.

The evidence is overwhelming; we have higher living standards, better clothes, houses and health care – and an abundance of material possessions and tools that no other age could have even imagined.

So why are we constantly told that the world is getting worse? What explains the constant flow of bad news? Why the pessimism in public discourse?

SO, WHY SUCH GLOOM?

In almost every country the vast majority of people continue to think that the world is getting worse. A 2016

YouGov poll asked people in some of the world's richest countries, if they thought the world was getting better or worse.*

Just 4 per cent of people in Sweden, 11 per cent of Americans, 3 per cent of Germans and 2 per cent in France thought things were getting better. A separate poll found that 92 per cent of Americans believed that global poverty is either getting worse or has remained the same.† Even in India and China, two countries in which progress has been particularly pronounced, almost half of people believe that things have got worse.

Maybe it's just that we are naturally pessimistic? Perhaps we are hardwired to always see the downside?

Could it be that assuming the worst gave our ancestors some sort of evolutionary edge? If you imagine the worst when it comes to whatever lies ahead, you might have a better chance of getting through it. Or perhaps our brains simply evolved to see the grim reality of the human condition as it actually was, over the course of many millennia?

Maybe there's more to persistent pessimism than all that, though. The way we look at the past is also shaped by our attitudes and outlook in the present. The idea of

---

*   See YouGov survey, January 8 2016.
†   See HumanProgress.org, Five graphs that will change your mind about poverty, March 17, 2017.

human progress – that we might today be better off than before – has, as we shall see, all sorts of implications. To avoid those implications in the present some prefer pessimism. If they can't quite convince us that we are all doomed, they settle for suggesting that things can't have got that much better since things really weren't all that bad before. But they were. And as a rule of thumb, the further back we go, the more grim the human condition.

2

THE WORST OF TIMES

Did the prehistoric people that once lived where my Essex vegetable patch now sits pass their lives living gently, in some sort of pristine primitive ideal? Did they gather what they needed to eat, and then idle away the hours in the healthy outdoors? It's quite a cosy idea, isn't it?

Ever since the eighteenth century, when French philosopher Jean-Jacques Rousseau (1712–78) pondered what primitive life must have been like, there has been no shortage of romantics who have imagined that early man lived at one with nature. There was, wrote Rousseau, 'nothing more gentle than [man] in his primitive state'.

A little more recently, Geoffrey Miller, author of *Spent*, portrays life for our hunter-gatherer ancestors as a sort of rural camping trip.* One endless summer of adventure, rather like an ancient version of *Swallows and Amazons*. The reality would have been more like *Lord of the Flies*.

NOTHING NOBLE
ABOUT SAVAGES

The twentieth century, you might imagine, was a uniquely bloody era in human history, with world wars and genocide. However, violent as it was, you would have stood a much greater chance of being a victim of violence if you had lived in any previous century.

Scientists have studied skeletal remains from the prehistoric past, from different locations around the world. The results suggest that in pre-state societies there were extraordinarily high levels of violence.

In Nubia between 12,000 BC and 10,000 BC, over half of all skeleton remains showed signs of a violent death. In parts of India between 2140 BC and 850 BC, over one-third seem to have perished through conflict.†

---

* See Miller, G., *Spent: Sex, Evolution and the Secrets of Consumerism* (2009).
† For more details about the historic decline in violence, see Pinker, S., *The Better Angels of Our Nature: Why Violence Has Declined* (2011).

The evidence of human savagery is grim and unrelenting. Recently in Germany, a Neolithic mass grave was discovered containing the grisly remains of twenty-six individuals showing evidence of violence – and possibly torture. Half a dozen of the victims were children.

Among some north American tribes in pre-Columbian times, there are estimated to have been 1,000 deaths from violence per 100,000 people per year. Among societies without a state, the average homicide rate was 500 per 100,000 per year. Almost 60 per cent of those who died in South Dakota in the 1300s were, it would seem, killed as a consequence of warfare and violence.

To put this into perspective, that would have made these pre-industrial societies more than twice as bloody a place to be as either Germany or Russia during the turmoil of the twentieth century.

Life in prehistory was, as the seventeenth-century English thinker Thomas Hobbes (1588–1679) put it, '… poor, nasty, brutish and short'. It's wishful thinking to believe otherwise. But that does not mean that there aren't many wishful thinkers around who, like Rousseau, imagine a non-existent idyll.

One brilliant illustration of wishful thinking about our prehistoric past came with the discovery of the remains of Ötzi, the so-called iceman, high up in an Alpine glacier on the Italian–Austrian border in 1991.

The discovery of this ancient corpse, preserved in the

ice for around four thousand years, prompted all sorts of speculation about the kind of Arcadian lifestyle he might have enjoyed. But Ötzi was not some sort of prehistoric hippy, enjoying a full-on organic existence.

Once researchers got around to examining his remains properly a darker story started to emerge. In 2001, a decade after his discovery, Ötzi underwent a CT scan and an arrow was found embedded in his back. He had head injuries and died due to violence. Further investigations then showed traces of human blood on his weapons, indicating that he might have killed a couple of people shortly before he met his own demise. Ötzi killed, and then in turn had been killed.

'A war of every man against every other man' – to use Hobbes' famous phrase – seems a pretty good way of describing what we now know about Ötzi's last few hours of life. But it was not just how Ötzi occupied his last few hours. Extreme violence seems to have been a way of life – and death – for many back then.

POOR FARMERS

The Central African Republic is today the poorest place on the planet. The average citizen of that country has to get by on not much more than a dollar or so a day. Yet before 1800, the average person almost anywhere would have been even worse off than that. Of course, it was possible to find a small number of people at the apex of certain societies who were rich – at times exceedingly so, having taken wealth off everyone else. But on average, people living before modern times lived in what we would regard as grinding poverty.

To get an idea of how poor most people were in most societies before the modern age, think of what life must have been like for millions in a place like Ethiopia, during the famine there thirty-something years ago. It was even worse than the Central African Republic right now. Starvation would have been a real risk; hunger common place; chronic malnutrition a fact of everyday life.

But surely, you might think, farming must have given people a steady food source? Once people learned how to grow their own food, they would have lived quiet lives of isolated self-sufficiency? Family groups would have tended the fields, enjoying an easy-going rustic life?

Actually, from the outset, life for farmers was tough. A number of historians have even suggested that while our hunter-gatherer ancestors were able to forage for what they needed with relative ease, the advent of agriculture left the first farmers worse off. A healthy, leisured, carefree existence in Eden, with everything on hand, apparently, was exchanged for one of unrelenting toil and drudgery in the fields.

This notion of farming as some kind of 'fall' isn't just

a narrative found in the Book of Genesis. It is a major theme of Yuval Noah Harari's bestseller, *Sapiens – a brief history of humankind*. Jared Diamond makes a similar point in *Guns, Germs and Steel*, when he calls the agricultural revolution 'the worst mistake in the history of the human race'.

Farming grain, it is implied, might have given us a more dependable supply of high calorie food, but it meant that we gave up the diet of Paleolithic purity that humans actually evolved to eat. In place of wild fruit and nuts – with a little lean organic fish and meat on the side – we took up a less healthy diet consisting of various forms of starchy stodge.

It's impossible to know if early farmers really did lead harder lives compared to those of their hunter-gathering forebears. Perhaps you can only insist hunter-gatherers had things better if you ignore the evidence of a lot of broken bones.

But what is clear is that life for the first farmers was certainly tough. For riding on the back of those that toiled in the fields have been various parasitic interests.

Harari calls farming 'history's biggest fraud' because, he suggests, although humans thought they were learning to live off other animals, various domesticated plants and animals were actually learning how to live off Homo sapiens. In a kind of reverse takeover, a few niche species of grain found in the Fertile Crescent spread to the far corners of the earth. Aurochs roaming the woodlands of Asia came to occupy countless fields across the planet as cows.

However, it was not so much other species that rode on the back of the first farmers, but other parasitic people.

OVERLORDS

Soon after the first people discovered that they could earn a good living by growing crops, others made a different discovery: they could earn a living by taking what those first farmers produced.

Not long after that, it was discovered that instead of simply plundering someone else's fields, resources could be extracted from farmers through a system of taxes, tolls and tyranny. The same grains that could be stored and exchanged by the first farmers could be demanded as tribute. With the agricultural revolution thus came the first centralized states.

Along the banks of the Euphrates, the Tigris and the Nile, the Yangtze, the Indus and the Ganges, emerged civilisations in which a caste of princes and priests lorded it over a mass of toiling peasants. Whether as serfs or slaves, those that worked in the fields were expected to hand over the lion's share of their crops to their overlords.

In almost every pre-modern farming society – from

medieval Europe and India, to Ming China and Mexico –
a strikingly similar extractive hierarchy emerged. From
one generation to the next, farmers paid extortionate
levels of tribute or taxation, often being left with only
just enough to feed themselves and their families – in a
good year.

According to Steve Pinker, homicide rates in human
societies tended to decline once some sort of centralizing
authority was established. It is arguable that with the
emergence of these patrician societies – something made
possible with the advent of grain farming – perhaps the
rates of violence declined. Still shockingly high by our
standard, this could conceivably mean at least some improvement in the human condition. Perhaps.

Maybe the warrior priests at the apex of such societies
did offer some measure of protection to the masses in
return for all those taxes, tolls and bonded labour after
all.

The reality is that far from setting humankind on the
road to perpetual progress, life for most within such
societies must have remained unrelentingly grim. Even if
having an overlord meant you were marginally less likely
to be attacked by an outsider, you still had to support and
submit to someone.

'Century after century the standard of living in China,
northern India, Mesopotamia, and Egypt hovered slightly
above or below what might be called the threshold of

pauperization,'* wrote the American anthropologist Marvin Harris in *Cannibals and Kings*. In such societies, 'total submissiveness was demanded of underlings, the supreme symbol of which was the obligation to prostrate oneself and grovel in the presence of the mighty'. Typically, a farmer in Ming China or medieval India would have had to hand over between 50 and 70 per cent of their produce.

Farming, in effect, allowed farmers to be farmed. Some have suggested that the human habit of farmer-farming actually led to a process of what you might call self-domestication.

The first animals our ancestors domesticated were dogs, something we appear to have done before we started farming. Farming, of course, saw us domesticate many other kinds of animal that we had previously been in the habit of hunting – aurochs and wild goats, sheep-like mouflon, wild boar and chicken-like jungle fowl. Each time humans domesticated an animal, a certain pattern of change occurred in the domesticated variant of the species.

The skeletal frame of the domesticated animal always became less robust and more gracile. The teeth and horns became noticeably less pronounced. The horns of the toughest bull on a contemporary farm are nothing like

* Harris, M., *Cannibals and Kings* (1977), p. 236.

those that existed on a wild aurochs. Infantile features – floppy ears in dogs, larger eyes – lasted longer into adulthood. Domesticated animals became much less aggressive than their pre-domesticated forebears. And, from dogs to sheep, their brains seem to have become slightly smaller.

Some scientists have noticed an almost identical pattern in the human anatomy, too. Compared to our archaic ancestors, our skeletal frames today are less robust. Our bodies are much less muscular and – perhaps surprisingly – our brain capacity is slightly smaller.

Whether it's possible to see all this as evidence of our self-domestication or otherwise, it is undoubtedly the case that a multitude of farmers, over many millennia, lived as little more than beasts of burden.

THE MALTHUSIAN TRAP

Long after humans discovered how to grow their own high-calorie food sources, most of those that worked the land continued to live a subsistence existence.

Incomes remained almost unchanged for centuries, as did life itself for most people. From what they used for shelter to food, from energy supplies to life expectancy, things stayed the same down the generations. A farmer in Egypt or China in AD 1500 would have had a living standard almost identical to a farmer living there in 1500 BC. The lifestyle of most people living in Elizabethan England would have been in many ways remarkably similar to that of someone living in England during the Iron Age.

Humans were, as that infamous eighteenth-century pessimist Thomas Robert Malthus (1766–1834) correctly spotted, stuck in a trap. Every time there was a technological innovation of some sort – iron tools or irrigation, windmills or waterwheels, new kinds of crops or new lands to farm – output increased. But so, too, did the number of people. Output per person remained essentially the same. As the economic historian Gregory Clark put it: 'In the preindustrial world, sporadic technological advance produced people, not wealth.'

The implication of this is that humans lived, for the most part, on just enough to get by. When food output fell for whatever reason, some people would have simply starved.

The grim logic of this meant that one of the only ways that a society could achieve an increase in output per person, albeit temporarily, was if a significant percentage of the population died off. This is precisely what happened, for example, in England after the Black Death, which caused the population to fall by almost half. Output per person increased afterwards since those that survived were left farming the more productive land.

Despite all the derision that has been heaped on the poor Rev. Malthus ever since he wrote his essay in 1798, his analysis – up until that moment – was basically correct. For most of human history, until about 1800, we were indeed stuck in a state of Malthusian misery.

Today, someone born in Britain can expect to live until they are over eighty. In China they can expect to be around until they are 76. Even in a less developed country like Ethiopia, life expectancy is now 65.

Had you, however, happened to be born in a farming community in Europe, Egypt or India over the three thousand years before about 1800, you would on average have been lucky to make it to the age of thirty. Infant mortality was staggeringly high, at around 30 per cent. Even if you survived childhood, you would have had siblings that didn't.

Childhood would have been marred by constant hunger. You would most likely be malnourished, to the extent that you would have been significantly shorter than your modern self had you made it to adulthood.

If you were a woman, when you made it to adulthood – if not a bit before – you would have produced a succession of babies, each one exposing you to an appallingly high risk of death during childbirth. Whatever gender, if you fell ill or had an accident, there were no modern medicines or anaesthetics to ease your pain and suffering.

Yet around about the time Malthus published what

has to be the most ill-timed essay ever written, something changed. Output started to rise faster than the population grew, worldwide. Today there are over six times more people living on the planet than there were in 1798, yet output per person is up sixteen-fold. Malthusian misery slowly started to recede in certain societies.

Why?

3

THE ENGINE OF PROGRESS

There is something appealing about the idea of self-sufficiency. Being able to produce all that we need ourselves seems so reassuring. Fed up with life in our cities and suburbs, a life of self-sufficient simplicity seems alluring. But to be self-sufficient is to be poor.

By definition, doing everything yourself means forgoing the efforts of others – and it is those efforts of others – provided to us through free exchange – that have elevated our standard of living.

CHICKEN SANDWICHES OR SELF-SUFFICIENCY?

The shortcomings of self-sufficiency were vividly demonstrated in a video posted online by a young American,

Andy George recently.* He set about trying to make for himself a chicken sandwich. Except he didn't just reach into the fridge for the bread, the tomatoes and lettuce, and the chicken breast. He decided he was going to make it all from scratch.

Firstly, he planted a vegetable patch to grow the pickle and salad and sowed the wheat for the bread. He travelled to the ocean to get seawater to boil for salt. He milked a cow to make the cheese and butter. He ground the flour to make the bread. Then he killed a chicken, before putting all the ingredients he had gathered together to make the sandwich.

All very wholesome and fulfilling perhaps. Except doing it all for himself meant it took him six months – and cost him US$1,500. Imagine what life would be like in a world where something as basic as a chicken sandwich cost about the same that we today pay for an iPhone Xs? Sandwiches would be a rare luxury, like caviar. Smartphones would be the preserve of billionaires and kings. We would all feel pretty poor.

Of course, if you or I today want a chicken sandwich, we need merely walk into a supermarket and buy one for what we could earn in ten to fifteen minutes on the minimum wage. Instead of having to do the whole

---

* See YouTube, How to make a chicken sandwich, part of the How to make everything series, published September 2015.

business of producing chickens, cheese, butter and all the rest of it, we can rely on the efforts of a network of others – and pay them from the proceeds of the specialized work – the job – we do.

From six months down to fifteen minutes. From US$1,500 down to a few dollars. Therein lies the difference between self-sufficiency and specialization and exchange.

Specialization and exchange are the essence of human civilization. It provides us not only with affordable food but enables us to escape the dawn-to-dusk drudgery our ancestors endured. Specialization and exchange give us time – to read novels or to write them, to patent inventions or play football. It is what has lifted our species from the swamp to the stars.

THE CIVILIZING EFFECT OF EXCHANGE

Specialization and exchange don't just make us materially better off. The interdependence that comes with it has helped civilize us.

As an animal species, we come into contact with unrelated strangers all the time – in supermarket aisles, on trains and in the cinema. For the most part, these encounters occur with no violence, and the occasional amicable interaction. It would be impossible to imagine almost any other animal species coming into contact with so many strangers, in such close proximity, without aggression and violence.

In our archaic past, people were – by modern standards – extraordinarily aggressive. Perhaps it paid to be aggressive to any unknown outsiders.

When we lived in small, self-sufficient communities, we held human life in low regard. As we have come to depend on an ever-widening network of specialization and exchange, we have increased our empathy for one another. The greater our interdependence on others, the greater our regard for others.

Once humans formed the habit of exchange and interdependence, aggression might not have been quite such a sensible default setting to survive – at least some of the time.

You don't need to look back to prehistoric times to see societies full of everyday violence. Using court and county records, the political scientist Ted Robert Gurr has calculated homicide rates in England since the Middle Ages. 'Merrie England' was in fact a rather murderous place. Oxford in the thirteenth century had a homicide rate three times above south-central Los Angeles at the height of the US crack cocaine epidemic of the early 1990s. The murder rate in England today is 95 per cent lower than it was in the Middle Ages.

Think of the most violent countries today: Colombia, with a homicide rate of 52 per 100,000 per year, or

South Africa, with a homicide rate of 69 per 100,000 per year. London in the fourteenth century was more violent than today. Italy and the Netherlands in the early fifteenth century had higher homicide rates than South Africa does now.*

Steve Pinker suggests that the rise of the market economy in Europe prompted a fall in violence from its Middle Ages levels, as commerce and interdependence brought about a change in cultural mores. Repeated transactions among trading partners encouraged trustworthiness. The more interdependent we have become, the greater has been the decline in violence, and with that a gradual shift in society towards gentler, less coarse manners and pastimes.

If the secret of human success is our interdependence – the habit we have of specializing and exchanging with one another – why did it not happen much faster? Why did it only generate a world of plenty in the past two or three hundred years, and not before?

THE EFFECT OF ISOLATION

Interdependence means exchanging with others – and perhaps in the past there just weren't many others to

---

* Pinker, S., *The Better Angels of Our Nature: A History of Violence and Humanity* (2012) p. 63.

exchange with? For much of our existence humans have lived in small, scattered groups, with little scope for interaction.

Twelve thousand years ago there were not many more than two million people alive on the entire Earth. That's equivalent to the population of Nebraska or Kiev spread out across an otherwise empty world. There would hardly have been enough people to exchange hand axes with, let alone chicken sandwiches.

Six thousand years ago, the population might have increased to about 30–40 million people, but that is still pretty sparse. It would be as if the only people alive on earth were Canadians, and they were scattered not only across the northern half of north America, but south America, Asia, Africa, Australia and Europe, too.

We know that by the Bronze Age the human habit of exchange was well established. Ötzi the Bronze Age man found in Alpine ice, for example, wore shoes that were so sophisticated and made from so many materials, it's hard to imagine that they were the product of any one person, but more likely the work of a specialist cobbler. If specialisation and exchange happened, why wasn't there more of it happening a lot sooner?

Matt Ridley puts forward the theory that isolation not only inhibits technological development, but societies cannot sustain more than the most basic level of technology unless they are interconnected. Citing the example of Tasmania, which became separated from mainland Australia at the end of the last Ice Age, Ridley argues that technology in Tasmania regressed.

Sure enough, it is after the advent of farming and the establishment of sedentary populations, and the emergence of the first city-states, that we start to see all sorts of inventions, from writing to the wheel.

Yet if isolation inhibited innovation and progress, it wasn't the only factor. Even after farming and the rise of cities, progress remained painfully slow. Per-capita output – be it in ancient Mesopotamia or pre-Columbian Mexico – were at subsistence levels even though people started to have more neighbours. Indeed, the number of neighbours increased in line with any growth in the food supply, which is why (almost) everyone remained poor.

EXTRACTIVE ELITES

Strictly speaking, 'feudalism' refers specifically to the social organization that existed in medieval Europe. In such a feudal society an aristocratic elite held lands in exchange for military service, while peasant farmers on those lands paid them homage, labour and a share of the harvest. The term has come to denote any set of social arrangements where a mass of peasant farmers provides their surplus to their overlords.

In that latter sense of the term, feudalism was the norm in most agricultural societies from the Neolithic age until the early modern era. From Laos in the Middle Ages to Buganda in the nineteenth century, we see the same essential arrangement of a small caste of warriors and priests ruling over a mass of farmers.

It was this parasitic arrangement that kept people poor.

Parasitic elites impoverished agricultural societies directly, by extracting from those that produced the wealth usually as much as they could. From Ming China to Mughal India, it was not uncommon for farmers to pay taxes, tolls and tributes that added up to between 40 and 60 per cent of their produce.

But there was a second even more important way in which overbearing elites kept the societies over which they presided poor. They denied those societies the gains that they might otherwise have had from specialization and exchange.

Under parasitic elites, resources within society were seldom allocated through free exchange. Normally economic resources exchanged hands because one party demanded them.

Under a system of spontaneous exchange, it's not just merchants and middle-men that do well. It's to the advantage of both buyers and sellers, who make the exchange in the first place because it leaves both better off.

Rather than allow such self-organizing systems of

specialization and exchange to evolve, with all the complexities involved, for most of human history small elites have used a combination of command and custom (social norms) to direct production – and to take their cut. They rigged things so that they could live at the expense of the productive.

The greatness of many 'great' world civilizations is often a measure of the success of an elite within those societies at extorting and expropriating from a mass of peasant producers – or simply biffing the neighbours. For many such civilizations, perhaps their achievement was their ability to last, something they achieved by changing little, as they replicated the same self-perpetuating stasis from one generation to the next.

Even when different dynasties came and went, for farmers on the banks of the Nile and the Euphrates, the Yangtze and the Indus, life in AD 1000 was pretty much what it had been in 1000 BC.

INHIBITING PROGRESS

Feudal societies stayed poor because the elites that presided over them inhibited free exchange, denying them all of the gains that might otherwise have flowed from it.

When redistributive exchange is used to allocate resources, it tends to hinder the most productive. If a farmer knows that he will have his grain taken from him, leaving him only the bare minimum required to feed his family, what incentive does he have to increase his yield?

In order to achieve intensive economic growth, with output rising per person, it is necessary to invest in order to expand production. A good harvest one year might give a farmer more time to clear some of the forest and increase the size of his field. Amazon today ploughs its profits back in order to expand the scope of what it sells. But what if you have a surplus-sucking elite hoovering up whatever it can? There is no surplus to invest – and therefore no chance of improved productivity.

Nor can an economic system based on custom, command and control generate the kind of complex supply systems needed to increase productivity.

Think back to our example of a humble chicken sandwich. If you buy one for lunch, you are in effect being fed because a lot of other people are working for you. In order to produce that chicken sandwich, an elaborate symphony of supply chains has had to come together. From the harvesting of the wheat, to the husbandry of the chicken, to the transporting, plucking, packaging, all kinds of efforts went into making such a sandwich. And it all had to happen with precision timing.

Everyone involved in each of those processes – even those working on minimum wages – did so voluntarily.

From the farmer who sold his grain to the shop worker who sold his labour putting the sandwich on the shelf, they served you because they stood to gain from doing so.

Imagine if instead it was all arranged by top-down direction and fiat? It would not take long before the complex supply chains started to break down. For most of human history, people have worked for other people not as willing providers of specialized services in a supply chain, but as supplicants, often acting in response to demands and under duress.

The sophisticated supply chains needed to produce even the most basic goods require free exchange. The tragedy for most of human history is that the parasitic have prevailed over the productive – and productivity per person remained constant.

Extractive elites at the apex of most settled societies have been hostile to free exchange – and indeed those that engage in it – to a greater or lesser degree. This is why specialization and exchange never developed in the way that they might have. Progress remained slow for as long as parasitism prevailed over production.

'Isn't that simplistic?' you interject. 'Not all economic interaction is either redistributive or mutual. Even in autocratic states, there must have been trade. Even in the most *laissez-faire* systems, there is redistribution.'

You are right. There's a spectrum – and along it, no society on earth has ever existed that managed to achieve authentically sustainable intensive economic growth by being on the redistributive end of it.

Just occasionally before 1800, however, there emerged a few societies in which the productive were no longer entirely at the mercy of the powerful. Specialization and exchange could reach beyond the provision of the rudimentary. In antiquity, among the republics of Greece, perhaps, and certainly Rome, and in the Middle Ages within the republic of Venice, as well as within the empire of the Abbasid in Iraq and the Song in China; and then in the sixteenth century within the Dutch Republic, there was a sustained increase in per-capita output. The motor of progress was allowed, for a few fleeting generations, to run free.

PART II

EARLY REPUBLICS

4

LIFT-OFF IN ANTIQUITY –
GREECE AND ROME

In April 480 BC the mighty Persian Empire invaded
Greece. It was an extraordinarily unequal contest – or
so it should have been.

Persia was not so much a super power, as a hyper-
power. Her empire stretched from the Indus to the
Aegean. Her emperor, Xerxes, commanded a vast pool of
manpower, making her invasion force one of the largest
ancient armies ever assembled.

And against her? The Greeks had no capital or unified
authority. They could field only a fraction of the number
of soldiers in the field, drawn from a mosaic of small
city-states and statelets, the loyalty of which was never
guaranteed. Not even Athens was able to impose a unified command.

For the Greeks, the situation that Spring must have seemed hopeless. For the Persians, their victory would have looked inevitable. Yet against almost unbelievable odds, the Greeks blunted the Persian onslaught. Then they defeated the invaders, first at sea at Salamis and then on land at Plataea, and the Persians retreated.

A hundred-and-fifty years later, the tables had turned completely. Under Alexander, the Greeks not only conquered Persia, but took Egypt, most of the Middle East and central Asia as far as India, too.

THE GREEK ACHIEVEMENT – MORE THAN MILITARY

The Greek achievement was not principally a matter of military conquest. In the century or so between driving the Persians from Greece and Alexander overrunning their empire, Greek culture flourished. The eastern end of the Mediterranean became in a way a Greek lake, her shores surrounded by cities with Greek-speaking communities, Greek culture, Greek learning and trade.

Alexander might have surged beyond the boundaries of Greece, conquering all before him, but what was far more durable than Alexander's fleeting empire was the way that Greek culture and ideas took root far from Greece – and flourished for centuries. Greek culture was perhaps the predominant way of life for many around the eastern Mediterranean for over a thousand years, until the Islamic conquests after the age of antiquity. Byzantium, which lingered on until the Middle Ages, did so as a Greek empire more than a Roman one.

In everything from art to architecture to philosophy and the way people thought, ancient Greece achieved the most extraordinary cultural innovations. The Parthenon is to this day regarded as one of the architectural pinnacles of humankind. Athenian philosophers laid the foundations for what we now think of as Western thought.

So much for the idea that there were only centuries of stagnation until the early modern era.

But what about economic, as opposed to cultural and artistic, achievement? Behind this aesthetic lift-off, might the economy of ancient Greece have been expanding?

Direct data about the performance of the Greek economy is almost non-existent. But there is evidence that hints at a significant expansion in wealth in the fourth and fifth centuries BC – material progress alongside all the other kinds. The population of ancient Greece increased three- to five-fold between 800 BC and 300 BC. Greece went from having a population density of about 3–5 people per square km to 12–15.

Not only did the population increase over this period without the normal Malthusian constraints kicking in. At the same time, living standards actually increased.

To be sure, historians today have little insight into the rates of Greek rents or taxes. But using guesstimates about what Greek city-states spent waging wars, and using what we know about the number of free citizens, it has been estimated that there was annual growth over a period of three or four centuries of between 0.01 and 0.07 per cent.

By the standards of today, such a per-capita increase might seem extraordinarily low. Even if we set such growth rates against those in early modern Europe, it's not much. But at the time, it was perhaps without precedent.

The archaeological record reinforces the idea of something exceptional happening, with steadily rising living standards and higher life expectancy. Houses got bigger and farms more extensive. Skeletal and dental remains suggest that people were in better health and that diet improved.

Athens under Pericles (461 BC–429 BC) was one of those rare and exceptional places where output increased faster than the population grew, making people on average much richer, or at least better fed. By the time that the Peloponnesian War broke out in 431 BC, Athens enjoyed a per-capita level of consumption similar to the level in Rome under Augustus (27 BC–AD 14).* In antiquity, the Roman Republic seems to have been the only other society

* Goldsmith, R.W., *Pre-modern Financial Systems: A Historical Comparative Study* (1987), p. 19.

to enjoy an increase in output that exceeded population growth.

ROME

At about the same time that the Greeks faced their Persian foe, in 496 BC on another Mediterranean peninsula – Italy – a small, unexceptional town was also locked in a deadly struggle against her larger neighbours, the Latin League. Outnumbered and betrayed by her former king – Lucius Tarquinius Superbus – Rome's army met her enemy on the shores of Lake Regillus. And crushed them.

The battle marked a key moment in Rome's rise. She went on to gain mastery over not just the Latin tribes of central Italy, but the whole Italian peninsula and, in time, a stretch of territory extending from Britain in the West to Iraq and Egypt in the East. Even by today's standards, with jet travel and email, that's a mind-bogglingly large territory for one city in Italy to control.

But there was much more to the Roman achievement than campaigns and conquest.

Ask any nineteenth-century historian to account for the predominance of Prussia in forging a unified Germany, and they will soon explain that Prussia prevailed not merely because of military victories – blood and iron – but economic take-off – coal and iron.

Talk to a foreign policy expert about America in the

world today and they will soon make the connection between the US as a military power and her economic strength, that underlies it. So why don't accounts of the rise of Rome focus on the economic ascendency of the city-state from the third century BC?

Partly because there's just not a lot of economic data. We know how much steel was being produced in nineteenth-century Germany or mid-twentieth-century America. We can't be so sure of the productive output of ancient Rome. But we do know enough to be certain that the Roman Republic achieved that rarest of things – output increasing faster than the population grew.

Between 300 BC and AD 14, the population of Italy approximately doubled, from four million to about seven million. If the Roman Republic had been stuck in the Malthusian trap, like most societies on the planet, output would have increased only in line with the population. But it didn't. While the population of Italy almost doubled over that time, total output almost quadrupled, meaning that wealth per person was twice as high. Economic historian Angus Maddison, with a precision that perhaps the data does not entirely justify, estimates that annual output per capita in Italy grew from the equivalent of US$425 in 300 BC to US$857 by AD 14.*

---

* See Maddison, A., *Contours of the World Economy 1–2030 AD* (2007).

This might not seem like a terribly impressive increase by today's standards. Average income per capita in Italy today is US$25,000 a year. But by historical standards, the level of intensive economic growth that Rome achieved was without precedent. 'Romans lived well,' writes Peter Temin in *The Roman Market Economy*. 'Better than any large group... before the industrial revolution.'

There might not be much hard evidence of economic output, but a pretty big clue as to what was going on has been found buried deep in the ice sheet in Greenland. Whenever humans smelt metals – especially tin, lead and silver – tiny microscopic amounts escape into the atmosphere. They are then blown far away, eventually settling back on earth. Some of these particles happened to land during a snowfall in Greenland all those years ago. And they remained trapped in the ice for millennia, concealed beneath countless later layers of snow.

When scientists drilled down into the ice sheet a few years ago, they found something remarkable and unexpected. The tiny traces of metal particles increased dramatically during the first, second and third centuries BC: clear evidence of increased human – Roman – industrial activity. Italy's wealth in the first and second centuries BC rose not as a consequence of conquest or booty, but thanks to higher productivity – more output per person.

DETERMINIST IDEAS ABOUT DEVELOPMENT

What was it that made the Greeks and the Romans so successful? At the time, many Greeks and Romans did what humans have so often done, and ascribed their wins to divine favour. Athens was uniquely blessed by Athena. Rome's victory over the Latin League was, apparently, due to the intervention of their gods, Pollux and Castor – who had appeared during the decisive moment in the battle beside Lake Regillus. In gratitude, a temple was built for them in the Forum.

It is not just the Romans who saw their success as a consequence of divine favour. This has been a remarkably persistent idea throughout history. Two-and-a-half thousand years on, the Victorian naturalist William Buckland was arguing that the enormous seams of coal that fuelled England's Industrial Revolution were a sign of divine favour. In nineteenth-century America, it was commonplace for politicians to talk of Divine Providence steering the republic towards a Manifest Destiny.

Divine determinism might have fallen out of favour more recently, but it's not the only kind of determinism on offer.

Running through Yuval Noah Harari's *Sapiens*, for example, is a strong streak of ecological determinism. Agriculture arose in certain parts of the world, he informs us, because that is where the kinds of species of plants and animals that could be domesticated happened to live. 'Those few species [suitable for domestication] lived in particular places, and those are the places where the agricultural revolution occurred.'*

We know that domestication, through selective breeding, changes the characteristics of crops and animals: grain husks become less fibrous; chickens lay more eggs; animals become less aggressive. Were the species we domesticated so domesticated because they were in some way suitable for farming? Or did they come to seem more suitable for farming through domestication? The determinists don't say. The possibility that domestication might have happened where it did because of characteristics in human societies, as opposed to those of certain plant and animal species, is left unexamined.

It is hard to see how ecological determinism can be used to explain the relative success of ancient Greece and Rome. Are we to imagine that they achieved intensive economic growth because they had access to better types of productive crops, compared to say the Persians or the Etruscans?

There is an even more elementary problem with ecological determinism. Proximity to more fruitful crops or fertile fields might have increased output in some societies, but

---

* See Harari, Y.N., *Sapiens, A brief history of humankind*, chapter 5, History's Biggest Fraud (2014).

it did not increase output *per person*. Nor does improved technology on its own mean higher living standards.

To be sure, the Greeks and the Romans achieved all kinds of precocious technological innovation – and such advances undoubtedly increased output. But so had all those other incremental technological innovations that had happened since metal tools started to replace stone ones at the end of the Neolithic age.

But better technology alone only increased output. Like having more productive crops and animals or fields, it did not necessarily raise output *per person*.

We know that when farming technology only produced low yields, population densities remained low. We know that the productivity of the land increased in areas that were naturally fertile – such as in certain river valleys – or when the application of new technology – such as irrigation – raised yields.

But we know, too, that the higher productivity of the land did not mean an increase in living standards; it just produced more people. Environmental factors and technology alone cannot account for increases in output per person. Something else explains increases in output per person: the division of labour. Greece and Rome achieved increases in output per person because they were open to increased specialization and exchange.

The default human condition has been for the productive to be at the mercy of the parasitic. The former has long kept the latter fed. The latter ensured that only the most rudimentary division of labour was possible – and everyone remained poor as a consequence. Progress and innovation occurred in antiquity when the human habit of innovation and exchange was able to happen unhindered; when the hold of the parasites was weakened – and on two peninsulas in the Mediterranean, the human propensity to specialize and exchange was allowed to kick in.

Being free from parasites means being independent – free from external extortion – but also being free from internal extortion. To flourish, the productive need to live in a society that is not only independent, but in one which power is dispersed as a constraint against home-grown, domestic parasites as well. And at the same time, a society needs to be sufficiently open to interdependence, so that it can interact and trade with the neighbours.

Independent, dispersed power internally, open to exchange with outsiders – notably these are precisely the conditions that one finds in ancient Greece and Rome for a few fleeting centuries. And in that brief moment, these societies thrived.

DISPERSED POWER

'Hold on,' you might interrupt. 'Far from Greece and Rome enabling the productive to escape the hold of the parasitic, aren't ancient Greece and Rome the epitome of parasitic societies?'

Warming to your theme, you might point out how both Greece and Rome ran empires that conquered and extorted. Each imported millions of slave labourers. How, you might ask, can that be squared with the idea that Greece and Rome arose on the back of free exchange?

It is absolutely the case that both the Greeks and Romans were, for much of their history extortionate powers. Under Alexander, the Greeks plundered their way across much of the known world. Rome was to become a military machine, fuelled by conquest and the extortion of provinces. In both societies, slavery – perhaps the ultimate parasitic behaviour – was commonplace.

But before they became empires that extorted, the Greek and Roman Republics enjoyed the conditions under which it was possible to achieve intensive economic growth.

It ought to be uncontroversial to point out that Athens and other Greek states, as well as the Roman Republic, managed to escape the attentions of various external predatory powers. The Greeks heroically repelled Xerxes; Rome saw off the Latin League in the sixth century BC, the Gauls (more or less) in 387 BC and Hannibal in 216 BC.

And at the same time as seeing off the external predators, Athens and Rome managed to keep their internal parasites in check, too. Greek city-states were not only independent from outside overlords; the different *poleis* were independent from each other, too. Ancient Greece had no capital or unified authority. No one state, not even Athens, was able to impose itself in perpetuity over the rest. Some 1,200 different *poleis* existed as independent entities between 650 and 323 BC. Greeks might have been united by a Pan-Hellenic identity and even mutual loyalty, which they showed when they joined forces as Greeks against a common Persian foe, as Herodotus tells us in his *Histories*, but they were independent from each other. Within the Greek world, political power was fragmented amongst a mosaic of states, in constant competition with each other. Power was not only dispersed among competing city-states, but within some of the most successful.

To be sure, plenty of Greek city-states were run by tyrants and kings. Others were oligarchies or plutocracies. But within some, power was dispersed amongst a few – oligarchies – or the people, the *demos* – democracies.

Of course, ancient Greek democracy was different to our own. Women and slaves had no say. The franchise was far from universal. But the key point is that in Athens, at the time of Pericles, power was vested in elected city officials, and exercised by those that answered for their actions to a diffuse set of interests.

Greek democracy might strike us as imperfect. But we need to try to look at the past without just reference to ourselves. Contrast the Greek system in the fifth and fourth centuries BC with the system of centralized monarchy in Persia, for example, where Xerxes and co. held absolute power.

Rome's republican constitution was, in the eyes of the contemporary Greek exile Polybius – living in Rome during the heyday of the republic – the perfect realization of Aristotelian political theory. That may be so, but precisely how and why the Roman system of republican government came into being is shrouded in myth and legend.

We know only the bare outline of what happened: having expelled her Tarquin king, Rome adopted a constitutional republic model that she was to retain for the next half-millennium. The Roman Republic was from then on ruled by an oligarchy of its most prominent families – the patricians – seated in the Senate. She was to have elaborate constitutional arrangements – and at times a measure of democracy – designed to disperse power.

From 494 BC, the common citizens – the plebs – gained a role in political affairs. From 367 BC, the tribunes had the power to veto laws made in the Senate. They were elected by the Tribal Assembly, in which the common citizens had a majority. The Lex Hortensia, passed in 287 BC, gave the decisions of the Tribal Assembly the force of law. The common citizens subsequently not only had a say in politics, nor did their tribunes merely have the power to veto the decisions of the Senate. From then on, they could make laws directly.

Rome was administered by magistrates, elected usually for a single year. Care was taken to restrain the power of whoever held office. There were two consuls elected to ensure that no one man or faction held too much power. Rome might have been an oligarchy, but it was an open oligarchy. Seated alongside the patricians in the Senate were the *equites*, or knights. They were often men who had made their fortune in business, and were in effect incorporated into the Senatorial elites. Many of Rome's leading heroes and statesmen – Cato the Elder, Marcus Cicero, Gaius Lutatius Catulus (naval hero of the Punic Wars) – were these new men, or *homines novi*.

Rome's institutions helped to hold power in check. An even more important constraint against the powerful, perhaps, was one of Rome's greatest innovations of all, the written law. Before 451 BC, Rome's laws had been a mixture of tribal custom and priestly command. But without writing them down for all to see, laws could be whatever the powerful wanted them to be. Half a century after expelling the last of the Tarquins, a written record of statute – the Twelve Tables – was drafted. It was to form the basic law of Rome for the next nine hundred years.

The written law was not just a constraint against arbitrary rule. It had the effect of secularizing the law.

The law in Rome after 451 BC was no longer the preserve of parasitic priests.

ANCIENT EXCHANGE

With internal and external parasites constrained, Greece and then Rome had the essential preconditions for progress. Is there any evidence that specialization and exchange followed? Yes, overwhelmingly so.

The Greeks traded far and wide – and relatively freely. They established colonies as far afield as southern Italy, Sicily, north Africa and the Black Sea.

The Athenian economy in particular was based on trade. With the land around her relatively unproductive, it was only through specialization and exchange that Athens was able to support and sustain the number of inhabitants that lived within her boundaries.

Athens encouraged trade, with other cities in Greece and far beyond. She imported wood from Italy and grain from Egypt. Athenian coins have been found as far afield as India.

Unlike her deadly rival, Sparta, who lived off her defeated neighbours, reducing them to the status of *helot* – a slave farmer forced to feed Sparta – Athens encouraged trade. Athens might have had slaves, too, but she also had a thriving market economy. There is some evidence that Athens possessed banks capable of conducting sophisticated transactions that allocated capital.

Certainly, what we know of Greek contractual law shows that the rights of merchants over property were safeguarded. Athenian merchants of the fourth century BC, like those of Rome later, were able to use loans to finance maritime trade and to do so with limited liability in case of shipwreck. Risk, in other words, could be correlated with reward.

There was not only an exchange of goods and services, but of ideas and technology. Athens and other city-states borrowed certain distinctive cultural features – many of which we now think of as definitively Greek (temples, statues, epic poetry and painted ceramics) – from others.

There is even more evidence of specialization and exchange in the early years of the Roman Republic.

New roads created a regional, rather than a purely local, market. Sea lanes, too, radiated out from Rome. Citing evidence from ancient shipwrecks, the Cambridge professor of ancient history, Keith Hopkins, argued that there was a surge in maritime trade beginning in the fourth century BC, with Rome at the centre of a Mediterranean-wide network. The volume of coins found by archaeologists and their widespread distribution – often long distances from where they were minted – gives a good indication that the economy was becoming increasingly monetized, with growing trade between different regions.

The low cost of transport encouraged regional specialization early on. By the middle of the third century BC, fine Roman pottery was being exported to Sicily, north Africa, Gaul and as far west as Cadiz. Rome also traded extensively with Athens, Alexandria and Antioch. During the late Republic, a factory system in Italy was producing pottery, arms, bricks, pipes, tiles and even textiles. Significantly, they were producing for a mass market, not just individual or local consumers. There was a standardized, mass-produced oil lamp, and red slip pottery. Wool weavers in small factories were selling to distant markets.

Roman law allowed bottomry loans – a kind of conditional loan whereby an investor funded a sea voyage on the understanding that if successful, they were entitled to a certain share of the profits. If, on the other hand, the ship was lost, those that had invested in the scheme would only have limited liability for losses. This encouraged investment.

Rome's constitution promoted voluntary exchange of not just capital, but also labour. 'Really? Weren't the Romans famous for taking slaves?' you might think. Yes, they were. Even in the early days of the Republic, before the first big influx of slaves that followed the acquisition of Sicily, not everyone could sell their labour voluntarily. But, alongside slavery, Rome had a free labour market. There was a mass of freehold farmers – the *assidui* – and an even greater number of *proletarii* – men who owned no property but were free to work as labourers, craftsmen and artisans, paid according to what they produced.

There were many independent producers in Rome, in stark contrast to the highly regimented economies of Egypt and the eastern Mediterranean at the time. Individuals in the East were deprived of the freedom to pursue personal profit in production and trade. Subjects of a king, they were forced to labour under a crushing burden of taxation, often dragooned to work in enormous collectives where they were little more than bees in a hive.

The Roman Republic was simply not like that. Far from collectivizing agriculture, it had a free market in grain, too. 'I thought Rome redistributed grain from the provinces to keep its own citizens fed?' you interject. 'Wasn't there a massive tribute paid by the subject provinces to the ruling Romans?' That was to come. But in the early days of the Republic, the vast quantity of grain imported into Rome to feed the city was purchased from willing sellers on the open market. Roman agriculture was efficient enough to feed a city of one million, easily the largest city ever to have existed until Beijing a thousand years later.

That agrarian efficiency released labour to live in the towns, further increasing productivity. The late Roman Republic and the early Empire had a level of urbanization not seen again until the eighteenth century. As the

German scholar F. Oertel put it, a Roman 'bourgeoisie came into being whose chief interests were economic'. A productive class, in other words, who could not easily be extorted and exploited by a class of parasites – helping to keep the system of free markets going.

For a few centuries, a society existed that achieved an increase in per-capita output or incomes, and a level of technological and cultural sophistication that was to remain unsurpassed for centuries. But, as we all know, progress stalled, and Rome regressed.

5

ROME'S REGRESSION

The collapse of the western half of the Roman Empire was perhaps the most dramatic – and bloody – regression in human history. A highly advanced, technologically sophisticated civilization, capable of sustaining a large, relatively literate and urbanized population came to an end. The population of Italy and the Western Roman Empire plummeted. Reading and writing were largely forgotten.

Efforts by revisionist historians to present the passing of the Roman order in the western end of the Mediterranean as some sort of genteel transformation between the third and fifth centuries are unconvincing. What happened was grisly, with an estimated death toll of about eight million. To put that into perspective, if a similar proportion of the human population were to have been killed in the mid-twentieth century, it would have meant the deaths of 105 million people – far more than were killed in the two World Wars combined.*

It would be a bit like our twenty-first-century Western way of life dramatically regressing back to how things had been in the fourteenth or fifteenth centuries – within the space of a few generations.

Roman civic order collapsed as warlords took over. Towns and cities emptied. A system of clearly defined laws was replaced by a world in which tribal custom – and the whim of the barbarian tribal chief – prevailed. But the barbarian invasions of the late fourth and early fifth centuries were ultimately a symptom of Roman decline, not a cause of it. The Romans had, after all, fought off far more organized foes, such as the Carthaginians.

The seeds of Rome's collapse lay not in the arrival of barbarian predators from outside the Empire, but was due to parasitic ones within.

PARASITES WITHIN

Long before the Roman Republic became an empire in 27 BC, power had become increasingly centralized. As

---

* Pinker, S., *The Better Angels of Our Nature: A History of Violence and Humanity* (2012), p. 195.

Rome acquired overseas provinces, she outgrew her system of checks and balances, allowing an oligarchy to emerge.

Vested interests within the Senate enriched themselves by systematically looting the provinces. Sicily's governor, Verres, personally made three million *denarii* during his tenure, which some have suggested exceeded the entire tax take of the island. Julius Caesar, while serving briefly as a Roman governor in Spain, managed to an enormous personal fortune, siphoning off for himself some of the profits from plunder. Others in the Senate grew rich from the proceeds of tax-farming businesses – *societates publicanorum* or *publicani* – which bid for the right to tax the provinces. Cicero estimated that, in his time, these *publicani* made average profits of 120 per cent.

A little like corporate banks today, these *publicani* enabled the state to spend right away, by providing investor cash up-front. Investors in the *publicani* were not, of course, issued with bonds. But like bondholders today, they were guaranteed a slice of future tax revenues. And, like the banks and government in our own time, there was a power nexus between the revenue-hungry government and *publicani*.

Publicani became a major investment vehicle for rich Romans, who bought shares in them. Investors were not disappointed. Having won the right to tax the provinces, the *publicani* systematically looted what they could.

In 133 BC, the king of Pergamum – a Greek city that controlled most of what is today western Turkey – bequeathed his kingdom to Rome. The *publicani* promptly set about stripping it systematically. According to the author of *Rubicon*, Tom Holland, 'The aim was not only to collect the official tribute owed... but to strong-arm the provincials into paying extra for the privilege of being fleeced.' Debtors might be 'offered loans at ruinous rates' in order to enslave him. 'Shipping sailed for Italy crammed with the fruits of colonial extortion.'*

There was a massive influx of slaves from Sicily and other newly acquired overseas territories. It was not unusual in the first century BC for ten thousand slaves to be auctioned at Delos in a single day. This huge supply of cheap labour helped further enrich the rich. Big landowners built up extensive farming corporations – the *latifundia* – using armies of slave labour. The freehold farmers could not compete. Many small independent farmers were forced to abandon the land, and drifted workless into the city. Rome, which started off as a society of freehold farmers, became a military machine, fuelled by external plunder and internal slavery.

In 104 BC, the plebeian tribune, Marcius Philippus, when proposing a law to redistribute land, claimed that

---

* Holland, T., *Rubicon: The Triumph and Tragedy of the Roman Republic* (2003), p. 42–3.

all the property in Rome was owned by fewer than two thousand people. His claim might have been an exaggeration but wealth had become greatly concentrated.

Maddison estimates that by the death of Augustus in AD 14, the elite – defined as Senators, *equites* and *decuriones* – comprised 121,600 people, out of a total Italian population of seven million. Yet, by that time they took over half of total income in Italy. This was an extreme concentration of wealth and far greater than exists in any contemporary liberal democracy. In fact, it was the kind of extreme level of inequality that one would have found in pre-revolutionary France in the late eighteenth century or Russia in the early twentieth. It was certainly very far removed from the old ideal of Rome as an agrarian republic of freehold farmers.

FROM REPUBLIC
TO EMPIRE

The increased concentration of power and wealth amongst a small elite provoked a crisis. Politics in the late Republic became a contest between rival interests battling over the spoils. There was, if you like, a first-century Roman version of our own twenty-first-century political populism. Things got so out of hand, they ended in civil war.

The plebs elected first Tiberius Gracchus – a kind of cross between Jeremy Corbyn and Donald Trump – and then his brother, Gaius, as consuls to take on the vested interests. Like those of the Left, the Gracchi brothers demanded more equality, land reform and a dole to help the poor. They also raged against cheap migrant labour.

The Gracchi tried to break up the giant *latifundia* farms. In 133 BC, Tiberius Gracchus advocated using the tax proceeds from Pergamum (King Attalus III had just died, bequeathing the whole of his unfortunate kingdom to Rome) to fund land redistribution, rather than simply funnel the riches into the hands of the elite via the *publicani*.

The response of the Gracchi to a system of provincial plunder which served to enrich a patrician elite was to demand that such proceeds be shared out with the plebs as well. And – despite both coming to a grisly end at the hands of patrician mobs – Tiberius and Gaius partly got their way. The corn dole that they instigated in 123 BC to feed the Roman poor remained in place until the very end of empire, and was even expanded as a form of welfare.*

---

* The corn dole was started by Gaius Gracchus, with the *Lex Sempronia frumentaria* providing for subsidized corn rations. It was not until the *Lex Clodia* in 58 BC that corn became completely free to its recipients. To the grain ration was added in time oil, pork, wine and even gifts of money.

But their achievement, in so far as they had one, was to ensure that it was no longer just the oligarchs that extorted the provinces. The poorer Romans joined in too. The corn dole that fed over a quarter of a million Romans a day by the time of Augustus was largely provided by Egypt – the personal possession of the emperor. Oppression and extortion of the provinces reached an epic scale.

After the Gracchi's demise, late Roman Republican politics continued to be dominated by the struggle between the elitist and populist factions – *Optimates* vs *Populares*; Sulla against Gaius Marius; Pompey vs Caesar. It was a conflict that ultimately destroyed the Republic.

The plebs might have got their dole, but the oligarchs prevailed. Sulla suppressed the plebeian faction and formally curbed the power of their tribunes. Democracy turned to oligarchy. The Republic had ceased to exist long before Julius Caesar formally overthrew it in 49 BC.

The Roman Republic – unlike Athens – never succumbed to external predators. She fell to a clique of powerful generals and politicians, whose fierce rivalry led them to ignore constitutional constraints. Members of the warring elite, Julius Caesar and Octavius, launched what was in effect a constitutional coup.

Efforts to restore the Republic (several emperors pledged to do it) were rendered meaningless because there were simply too many vested interests in the imperial order – from Pretorian guards to rich Senators.

At the battle of Actium in 31 BC, one of the warring oligarchs, Octavian, defeated his rivals. Calling himself Augustus, the *princeps* – or 'the first' – he established a military dictatorship. His successor, Tiberius, abolished the plebeian assembly. It might have been a relatively benign military dictatorship at first but power was now in the hands of one person, who more often than not asserted his claim to the job through force. The constitution Polybius described in such detail in the second century BC had gone forever – and with it the genius of Roman civilization.

The problems that the centralization of power was to produce were not immediately apparent. In fact, Roman grandeur was all the greater once she became an imperial power. Given the violent disorder that had gone before, the rule of Augustus, even in the eyes of Republican traditionalists, must have seemed like an improvement. Augustus encouraged trade and abolished tax farming – making the collection of taxes less arbitrary and less of a disincentive to commerce.

The early Empire, wrote the Russian historian Michael Rostovtzeff, was a period of 'almost complete freedom for trade and splendid opportunity for private initiative'. But with power so centralized, the seeds of destruction had been sown. Stagnation set in slowly. According to the economic historian Raymond Goldsmith, there is 'no evidence of an upward trend in income per head over the first two centuries of empire'.*

REDISTRIBUTION

Under the Empire, Italy no longer lived through mutual exchange by trading with far-flung parts of the Mediterranean. She became a parasite, living increasingly off redistribution. The Empire became a military machine, which needed feeding. This was done partly through conquest and plunder – the Roman Empire expanded to reach its greatest territorial extent under Trajan (AD 98–117) – and partly by pauperizing the provinces.

But whatever spoils it might have yielded in the short term, redistribution couldn't sustain the growth produced by mutual exchange. Intensive growth didn't just stop; it went into reverse. The military machine of empire put constant upward pressure on taxes. Extortionate taxes often became simple extortion. Caligula achieved what the Gracchi had failed to do when he seized the estates of many of the richest Roman landowners.

Property rights became progressively less secure, as confiscation became an established practice. Increasingly,

* Goldsmith, R.W., *Pre-modern Financial Systems: A Historical Comparative Study* (1987), p. 35.

big fortunes were not made through mutual exchange, or selling to a market, but by being the beneficiary of one of the increasingly frequent rounds of land expropriation. Wealth was increasingly concentrated. Goldsmith estimates that the wealthiest 3 per cent in Italy accounted for a quarter of all income.*

A change of emperor could mean the sudden loss of a family estate. Or, if you backed the right horse, gaining one. Many of the elite, therefore, had a vested interest in the imperial succession. Perhaps unsurprisingly, contests to succeed to the purple became increasingly violent. From AD 180 on, it was rare for an emperor to die peacefully.

Pressure to provide money to the army was unrelenting. So much so, in fact, that Nero took the decision to debase the currency, reducing the silver content of the *denarius* to 90 per cent. Cutting the amount of silver by 10 per cent meant that the authorities were a little better off for every debased coin they issued – and the person who received that coin, 10 per cent worse off. It was a way of transferring money from the citizen to the state.

To help pay for a vast military machine, Roman emperors routinely debased the currency by reducing its silver content. Emperor Trajan reduced the silver content to 85 per cent; Marcus Aurelius (AD 161–180) to 75 per cent.

---

* Goldsmith, R.W., *Pre-modern Financial Systems: A Historical Comparative Study* (1987), p. 36.

By the reign of Septimus Severus (AD 193–211), it was down to 50 per cent. By the middle of the third century, 5 per cent.

This debasement of the Roman currency caused massive inflation. By the reign of Diocletian (AD 284–305), prices were rising so fast that he issued an edict to try to control the price of many goods throughout the Empire. Like our own elites, that of Rome not only manipulated the money supply to enrich a few, they also started issuing cheap credit. Tiberius gave out low-cost loans to crony companies involved in public works projects.

Rome ultimately became an economic empty shell, receiving taxes, grain and goods from the provinces, but producing almost nothing herself. 'The mob of Rome and palace favourites produced nothing, yet continually demanded more, leading to an intolerable burden on the productive classes.'*

Marine archaeologists have recovered the remains of shipwrecks which carried cargoes around the Mediterranean in antiquity. Dating the wrecks and then counting the number from different centuries has given archaeologists a crude indicator as to the volume of sea trade at any particular time. Using this system [of measurement], it was seen that there was a dramatic decrease in

* See essay 'How excessive government killed ancient Rome', Bruce Bartlett, Cato Institute.

seaborne traffic at this time. Trade seems to have dried up and goods were transported only according to central command and under duress, not traded freely. No longer trading with others but extorting from them, and without a sound currency to underpin trade and investment, Italy de-industrialized. The factories that had existed in the first century BC were gone by the third century. There was no longer a mass market for many goods as there had been. In the Western Empire – the Eastern part seems to have fared better – regional specialization and exchange dried up.

Again, evidence from the Greenland ice cores – showing a fall in the amount of lead and silver released into the atmosphere – testifies to this industrial decline. Manufacturing did not return to the level it had reached in the first century AD until the thirteenth century.

Romans had once been innovators, capable of taking new technology and using it to great effect. It is striking that there was an almost total absence of technological innovation during the period of Empire. Businesses, which had been in private hands, were increasingly corralled into '*collegia*' – cartels. Workers were organized into restrictive guilds. By the third century AD, there was no longer a free labour market. Imperial decrees forbade workers from changing jobs or moving from one workplace to another – something that, in the first century AD, only slaves were prevented from doing.

Trade fell precipitously, and inflation in the third century AD is estimated to have been 15,000 per cent, making monetary exchange increasingly difficult. With the monetary economy breaking down, normal taxation became harder and harder to levy. The Roman state began to demand taxes in the form of goods and services. The tax contribution, moreover, was calculated according to military need.

This was not the only way in which the late Roman economy began to take on many of the attributes of feudalism, long before any Goths showed up. Agricultural workers became semi-servile *coloni*. Like slaves, they were increasingly bound to the land and to a landlord. As this proto-feudalism took hold, they were, like vassals, prevented from selling their own property without their landlord's permission.

With ruinous tax rates, little incentive to trade and few gains to be had from specialization, landlords turned their estates into increasingly self-contained units. Self-sufficiency might have been essential, but it meant doing without the gains in output per person that had created such wealth in an earlier age. Italians became much poorer.

To grasp the full scale of this economic calamity, consider the fact that, by AD 400, the number of people living on the Italian peninsula had plummeted by about a third, from seven million in AD 14 to five million – the lowest number since 200 BC. This decline happened *before*, not as a consequence of, the barbarian invasions.

'It is clear,' writes Maddison, 'that there was a significant decline in per-capita income in all the west European provinces.' In fact, income per capita in Italy in AD 400 fell back to where it had been in 300 BC, *700 years before!* The economy had returned to localized self-sufficiency.

As the Belgian medievalist Henri Pirenne puts it, with the end of trade, specialization and exchange, 'the minting of gold had ceased, the lending of money at interest was prohibited, there was no longer a professional class of merchants, oriental products… were no longer imported, the circulation of money reduced to a minimum… Civilization had regressed to the purely agricultural.'*

By the time that those external predators – the Goths and the Vandals – showed up, they were helping themselves to what Rome's own parasites had left behind.

For the following six centuries, there is little evidence of any increases in per-capita income or output anywhere in Europe. As we shall see, what increases there were in terms of per-capita income or output occurred elsewhere. But then from about AD 1000, an extraordinary society emerged off the coast of Italy: Venice. It, too, was a republic, and her economic achievement is also a measure of how effectively she managed to disperse power internally.

* Pirenne, H., *Mohammed and Charlemagne* (2001), p. 242.

6

VENICE – A MIRACLE ON
A MUDBANK

Try to imagine the most unpromising piece of real estate on which to establish a society that might prosper. You would struggle, perhaps, to pick a worse spot than a water-logged island off the northeast coast of tenth-century Italy. Yet amid the chaos and collapse that followed the fall of the western half of the Roman Empire, that is where a small community was established on 25 March AD 421, according to legend. The swamp seemed to offer relative safety and security, if little else.

THE SERENE REPUBLIC

Venice was literally built in a backwater, with almost

no farmland and few natural resources, besides sea salt and a few fish. Out of the lagoon emerged between the tenth and thirteenth centuries what Julius Norwich calls 'the richest and most prosperous commercial centre of the civilized world'. Venice stands out as being the only society in Western Europe, indeed perhaps anywhere, that achieved a sustained increase in per-capita output and income between the collapse of the Roman Empire in the west, and the emergence of the Dutch economy in the early modern era.

The Venetian Republic in the early Middle Ages was an extraordinary achievement. She was in so many ways precociously modern; her constitutional arrangements included a complex system of checks and balances, and laborious due process. She was by the standards of the day tolerant, trading with the Muslim world – often in defiance of papal edicts – and relatively open to Jewish communities – albeit with intermittent periods of persecution.

The state granted merchants the right to trade through the allocation of *commenda* contracts. These limited the liabilities for merchants. Unlike the granting of monopolies and other trade privileges in other European towns at the time, it seems that *commenda* contracts were allocated if not to anyone that wanted one, then certainly to a wide range of entrepreneurs and merchants. You did not need to be in the business of bribing the king in order to be allowed to trade. The *commenda* contract system seems to have encouraged open competition, rather than imposing restrictions.

The population of Venice grew rapidly. By 1050, what had been a fishing village a couple of centuries before was now home to about 45 thousand people. By 1200, she was a city of 70 thousand. Before the Black Death, in the mid-fourteenth century, her population had swelled to over 120,000. To an even greater extent than ancient Athens, Venice was quite unable to feed herself from what she grew.

Like Athens, she sustained herself through trade. Her population not only grew, but those that lived there lived better. Output per capita in Venice was far higher than anywhere else on the planet. She shone while all around her the Mediterranean was a sea of Malthusian gloom.

Intensive growth allowed Venice to punch above its weight. Despite being a tiny city-state 0.0005 per cent the size of the Holy Roman Empire and 0.0001 per cent the size of the Ottoman domains, Venice was often a match for these parasitic powers around the Mediterranean. Indeed, in 1204 she notoriously spearheaded the attack on Constantinople, when her aged Doge, Enrico Dandolo, led the first successful assault on the walls of that great city in almost a thousand years.

How did she do it? The Venetians themselves attributed their successes to the blessing of their patron, St Mark.

But it wasn't divine determinism that accounted for her success.

INDEPENDENT, NOT ISOLATED

Venice was secure from external predators. Those muddy islands might have seemed an unlikely place to want to live, but the neighbourhood across the water was far worse. Venice's almost impregnable lagoon protected her from marauders and invasion. It saved her from the Longobards, then Pepin and the Franks. It kept out the Huns and the Saracens (whose fleet once got to within sight of the city). It stopped the Normans far more effectively than any city wall.

But it was not just geography that kept predatory powers at bay. Venice had the great fortune to have been born – notionally at least – a child of Byzantium. She was, at one time, the most western point of that empire. This kept her free from the feudalism of the mainland, and beyond the reach of the Holy Roman Emperor. At the same time, she was overlooked by the distant court in Constantinople, and was outside any meaningful kind of imperial control. By AD 810, Venice was in effect independent – and from then on, she was able to avoid getting gobbled up by any of the big power blocs around her.

But even though she was an island, Venice was never

insular. Her barges filled the waterways of northern Italy and the Adriatic. Because she began as a Byzantine province, Venice was born part of a wider Greek-speaking Mediterranean world. In other words, Venice networked with her neighbours. Even by modern standards, a very high proportion of economic activity in Venice was linked to trade, suggesting a high level of specialization and exchange.

The city grew rich trading spices and manufactured Byzantine wares from the East. She gained trading rights in Constantinople and established a large Venetian quarter there. By 1140, she was importing raw cotton from the East, processing it and exporting it to be sold in Alexandria, Constantinople and Jerusalem. Trade functioned as an extension of Venice's resources. It allowed a few acres in an Italian lagoon to draw on the grain of the Po Valley, the timber of Dalmatia, the vineyards of Apulia, sugar and cotton from Cyprus, silk from China and the metalwork of Constantinople.

DISPERSED POWER

Independence and interdependence aren't enough alone to account for Venice's economic miracle. The serene republic owes her success to a further factor: she was free from internal parasites, too. Venice might have been an oligarchy – never a democracy – but for her first few centuries, power was dispersed amongst a merchant aristocracy. Think of Florence, and the name Medici comes to mind. The Sforza family are synonymous with medieval Milan, the Este with Ferrara and Modena, the Scaligeri with Verona. But there is no equivalent family in Venice. To be sure, there were plenty of distinguished Venetian families, like the Dandolo or Morosini, who produced plenty of heroes, villains and statesmen. But no single family or faction dominated in quite the way that the Medici and the rest did in other city-states.

In most northern Italian towns, the republican theory of the communes was soon subverted by tyrannical reality. *Il signori* took over. Yet when, in 1032, Domenico Orseolo attempted to set himself up as a Venetian *signore*, he was ousted. Tellingly, his replacement, Domenico Flabonico, was a silk merchant with staunchly anti-dynastic views. 'Although they are few compared to the whole population of the city,' observed the fourteenth-century jurist Bartolus of the Venetian aristocracy at the time, 'they are many compared to those ruling in other cities.'

After the attempted coup of 1032, on only two occasions over the next 700 years did the same family name appear consecutively on Venice's long list of doges. The power of the Doge – who henceforth was elected by the General Assembly, and subsequently a Ducal Assembly – was progressively eroded. Doges could no longer appoint cronies to any of the offices of state. Each new doge was required to sign a binding '*promissione*' contract before assuming office, which, in evermore elaborate terms, stipulated things they could no longer do.

The Venetian constitution was complex and elaborate, at times to the point of near absurdity. But it kept power diffuse. The Doge was held to account and answered to the merchant interest. Neither the Doge, nor the Great Council, nor the Venetian Senate could make decisions without the approval of the others. Venice, almost uniquely in the medieval Mediterranean, had independent magistrates, courts and courts of appeal, as well as the rule of law.

The dispersion of power and the supremacy of mercantile interests amplified the gains of interconnection. They made the city an attractive trading hub. They facilitated voluntary exchange. By the late tenth century, the merchants had pushed successfully for a policy of free trade with Byzantium. They sought – and won – tax exemptions on Venetian goods from the Holy Roman Empire and Otto III. They even traded openly with the Saracens in north Africa.

Being independent, Venice could ignore the papal edicts banning trade with Muslims, as well as the ones that tried to outlaw charging interest on loans. When two producers controlled the market in tiles, cement and building material, the government broke up the duopoly and sold off the kilns. The Senate investigated unfair practices in the cotton trade with Cyprus. No one family was allowed more than one member on the key administration boards. As well as ensuring competition, Venice's government was, as historian Frederick Lane puts it, 'frankly and efficiently capitalistic'.

Venetian law actively encouraged exchange and early capitalism. *Colleganza* or *commenda* contracts, not unlike the system of bottomry loans in ancient Rome, allowed investors to put private capital into trade missions almost as a sort of *ad hoc* joint-stock company. They gave investors a measure of control over the venture into which they were putting their money and limited their liabilities.

Commenda contracts were so successful that they did not just facilitate private capital investment in private enterprise, but also allowed a measure of social mobility, reflected in official records of new investors. According to surviving government documents from the time, in 960 and then again in 982, between 65 per cent and 81 per cent of those acquiring a *commenda* contract were doing so for the first time.*

Independence from external parasites and dispersed power to safeguard against internal ones, plus interdependence with the neighbours – we can be certain that

* Acemoğlu, A., and Robinson, James A., *Why Nations Fail: The Origins of Power, Prosperity and Poverty* (2012), p. 153.

these three magic ingredients are essential for intensive economic growth. Not merely because of what happens when they exist. We can also see what happens when they cease to exist: regression.

7

HOW VENICE SANK

Giorgia Boscolo became Venice's first female gondolier in 2009. Breaking with centuries of tradition, 34-year-old Giorgia was finally allowed to do something previously only men had done – ferry paying customers around Venice's waterways.

A triumph for feminism, you might think? Only sort of. Giorgia was only allowed to paddle a gondola on certain days of the week, provided no male gondolier was available to do the job. Other women who have since tried to take the test needed to qualify for a licence have complained that the male examiners were 'overly strict' in order to keep them off the canals.

It's easy to read this story as a clash between twenty-first-century egalitarianism and quaint Venetian tradition. Except Venice was never traditionally in the business of restricting trade like this. When Venice was the wheeler-dealing capital of the world, there was no guild of gondoliers. Guilds only became compulsory in Venice in 1539. Those rules and regulations that stipulate who can row what kind of gondola, built to what specification and under what conditions, aren't as old as we imagine.

At some point, the productive – long paramount – had been made subservient to a parasitic interest. This subtle, yet profound, shift turned what was once the centre of innovation, ambition and enterprise into a crumbling museum.

A SUBTLE SHIFT

How did it happen? The change was not dramatic. There was no sudden transformation, followed by a swift collapse. Decline by its nature tends to be a slow, steady rot. Indeed, in terms of art and architecture, Venice's most lavish and exuberant decades happened only after a gilded – or should that be 'guilded'? – elite had taken over. Like Medici Florence or imperial Rome, perhaps it takes the proceeds of parasitism to commission the greatest art.

Like Rome, Venice was also a republic that acquired an empire. The great inflow of wealth from overseas possessions upset the republic's internal equilibrium. It was not so much the raw inequality that was problematic but the fact that this new source of wealth allowed a faction within the body politic of the Republic to outgrow and circumvent the safeguards against the predominance of any one group.

After sacking Constantinople in 1204, Venice took over various prize territorial possessions in the eastern Mediterranean that had previously belonged to Byzantium. A new class of colonial administrators grew rich running them. Trade from Cyprus, especially from sugar produced on slave estates, enriched a small number of families. Much as the acquisition of Sicily and Pergamum had enriched a faction within the Senate, a small number of Venetians benefitted from the acquisition of these new imperial possessions.

At the end of the thirteenth century, a rich clique within Venice launched a constitutional coup. Previously an open oligarchy, in 1297 there was what is known even today as *Serrata* or closure, after which membership of the Great Council was restricted to political insiders. Soon membership became hereditary *de jure* as well as *de facto*.

A new executive body, the Council of Ten, was created in 1310. It became the chief executive and judicial body of the state, answerable only to itself. Centuries of trying to restrict the danger of an overbearing executive by constraining the Doge were undone. From 1315, the merchant aristocracy became a closed shop, literally. If your name was registered in the *Libro d'Oro* – or Gold

Book – you were part of the oligarchy and could hold office and take part in administrative matters. If you were not on the list, you were not allowed in.

And you were not just excluded politically, but economically, too. The number of *colleganza* contracts involving non-nobility – those not named in the Gold Book – dramatically declined. Economic historians Diego Puga and Daniel Trefler have shown that before the *Serrata*, between 1073 and 1203, 40 per cent of those involved in *colleganza* contracts in the city were not nobles.

Between 1221 and 1240, a small majority of non-nobility engaged in *colleganza*-based trade. But after the oligarchic coup, the proportion of commoners trading under *colleganza* contracts fell dramatically. Between 1325 and 1330, a mere 5 per cent were non-nobles. Between 1339 and 1342, none.

Clearly, a few rich merchant families started to use political connections to ensure that *colleganza* contracts were only awarded to the well connected. Within what was once a freewheeling city-state, guilds emerged, and they entered into a symbiotic alliance with the powerful and well connected, agreeing to pay a galley tax in return for restrictions on trade that suited them.

In 1324, the *Capitulare Navigantium* law entered into force, stopping poorer merchants from trading. From then on, only the rich and politically-connected were able to engage in long-distance trade and commerce. Indeed, the parasitic would force the productive to carry them – literally. Rules were imposed on private carriers requiring them to have a noble on board, who was automatically granted a certain amount of stowage space for goods traded in his own name, even if they were carried at someone else's cost.

Alongside the internal restraint of trade, the elites imposed protectionism. Statutes were introduced preventing foreign-born merchants – and their capital – from investing in *colleganza* ventures. By the fifteenth century, rules insisted that Venetian goods had to be carried on Venetian ships. A series of evermore protectionist Navigation Acts followed.

And with protectionism came nationalization. From 1325, galleys had to be publicly owned, with merchants bidding to have space aboard them. Somewhat like our regulated markets today, trade still happened, but it was increasingly based on obtaining permission. Relations with officialdom in the naval yard and industrial hub of the city, the Arsenale, suddenly became more important than those with customers – who were forced to buy from a restricted range of suppliers.

But, as a manufacturing hub, the Arsenale became a shadow of its former self. In the early fourteenth century, it had been the largest industrial centre in Europe and the site of innovation in ship design. But soon it was producing only a few dozen antiquated galleys totally unsuited to carrying goods on the long-distance ocean routes that the Dutch and English had opened up.

Indeed, far from trying to adapt to the new nautical technology that was transforming shipping in north-western Europe, Venice's rentier rich restricted innovation. Ship construction in the Arsenale was nationalized shortly after the *Serrata*. While new, faster, ocean-going ship types were designed and built in Holland and England, such as the Dutch *fluyt*, the Arsenale continued to churn out the same sort of ponderously slow, less manoeuvrable galleys. Perhaps with only one state-owned boat-builder, there was simply not the scope for the kinds of innovations happening elsewhere.

Venetian naval technology might have been sufficient to defeat the Turks at Lepanto in 1571, when galleys were pitched against galleys. But north-western Europe had by then developed an entirely new kind of naval technology, with ships able to undertake long-distance ocean voyages, all of which left galleys, partly powered by rowers, increasingly obsolete. 'The *Serrata*,' say Puga and Trefler, 'marked the beginning of the end of Venice's maritime power.'

CRONYISM

Venice's slide from free-market capitalism to crony corporatism brought restrictions on manufacturing and labour, too. Before the thirteenth century, guilds had been expressly forbidden from boycotting customers and had never been permitted to exclude new workers from joining.*

That all changed long before Giorgia Boscolo had had the temerity to want to row a gondola. Guilds became compulsory and they were no longer open to anyone. They acted as a restraint on trade – as Giorgia was to discover – in the interests of allowing a privileged few a means of earning a living free from competition.

By the fifteenth century, there were detailed rules specifying what kind of apprenticeships textile workers had to have undertaken, and restricting who could work and in what capacity. Increasingly, Venetians were no longer free to sell their labour to whom they wished. In fact, workers even lost the right to leave. Skilled craftsmen of the Murano glassworks and shipwrights of the Arsenale were forbidden from emigrating. In 1460, it was decreed that caulkers attempting to leave Venice to sell labour elsewhere were liable to face six years in prison.†

The result of these constraints was that Venice lost her innovative edge – and not just in ship-building. In the sixteenth century, for example, silk merchants imposed

* A statute of 1219 specifically forbade guilds from price-fixing and other restrictive practices.
† Cipolla, C., *Before the Industrial Revolution: European Society and Economy 1000–1700* (1993), p. 189.

restrictions on silk processors in order to protect their own interests – but in doing so, prevented Venice's silk looms from developing new techniques.

In the absence of opportunities for productive investment, the elite increasingly ploughed their capital not into trade or manufacturing, but into large estates on the *terra firma* mainland. So much so, in fact, that in 1677, a law was passed to try to stop this from happening.

Under the weight of parasitism, innovation gave way to stagnation. Once a place where outsiders came to make their fortune, Venice became a city where 'every man owed his position to what his father had been, from *stevedore* to customs house, through to the privileged craftsman of the Arsenale, and the secretariat in government bureaus up to nobles in the Senate and the Council of Ten'.*

Venice's increasingly closed oligarchy did not content itself with simply restricting trade in order to feather its own nest. They also helped themselves to public money. Bureaucracy expanded to provide employment to the well connected. A law passed in 1490 seems to suggest that most of the nobility in Venice by that time were living on the public payroll, enjoying some sort of sinecure. Sinecures permeated the Arsenale and the military, rendering both increasingly ineffective. The American

---

* Lane, F.C., *Venice: A Maritime Republic*, p. 427.

medievalist Frederick Lane blames the string of naval and military defeats that Venice suffered on the incompetence of over-promoted oligarchs.

Within what had been a relatively open and meritocratic republic emerged a class – the *Barnabotti* – that lived off state sinecures. Not unlike the class of quangocrats in Britain today who earn a good living from the public sector, they lived well at public expense – and had a vested interest in an enlarged state.

The *Barnabotti* started to consume a growing share of the state budget. By the seventeenth century, they accounted for over 200,000 ducats of state spending each year. In the last days of Venice as an independent state, more nobles were on the state payroll than there were members of the Grand Council.

To fund the sinecures, the parasites had to take from the productive. So, taxes – sometimes in the form of forced loans imposed on Jewish merchants – soared. In 1340, tax revenues yielded 250,000 ducats; 1.15 million ducats by 1500 and 2.45 million ducats by 1600. Unlike the Roman elite, the Venetians did not bother with debasing the currency. They simply imposed forced loans on those who were not politically well connected through a sort of compulsory bond-purchase scheme.

The guilds, too, became a kind of tax-farmer for the state. Once required to provide the government with a compliment of galley rowers in times of crisis, the guilds began to pay a *galeotti* levy in lieu of this, which morphed into a tax. Perhaps it was in return for this that the guilds got rules and regulations that protected their interests.

The enrichment of the Venetian elite was not down to the free market. On the contrary: a small elite enriched themselves by restricting the market. In fifteenth-century Venice, capital was concentrated as a consequence of crony corporatism.

THE END OF THE REPUBLIC

From the sixteenth and seventeenth centuries, Venice lost her share of the market in Mediterranean textiles. The Dutch and the English producers simply undercut what Venice sold. The advent of Dutch and English competition might explain how Venice fell behind, but not why. The reason Venice's textiles were so hopelessly uncompetitive – why no Venetian producer, despite the head start of several centuries, was apparently capable of making the sort of innovations in textile production that seemed to come so easily to her rivals – was, in large part, due to the restrictive practices of her guilds. Cronyism killed off her competitive advantage.

Venice stagnated, declining not necessarily in absolute terms, but certainly in relative terms. Other cities and states in Europe became more important centres of trade, production and innovation. She became an economic sideshow and, increasingly, a relic.

In 1796, several centuries after the *Serrata*, Napoleon finally did what no invader had achieved in a thousand years – he launched a successful invasion across the lagoon. Venice, an independent state for over a thousand years, was annexed by outsiders.

In a sense, the real Republic had fallen long before. What Napoleon snuffed out was a grubby rentier state, not the proud hub of innovation and exchange that had dominated Mediterranean trade in the Middle Ages. If few rallied to defend the Republic when the end came, perhaps it is because there wasn't much of a Republic left to defend.

Maybe the time to defend the Venetian Republic had been long before, at the time of the *Serrata*. That, at least, was the view of one Bajamonte Tiepolo, who led a populist revolt against the increasingly self-serving oligarchy in the summer of 1310.

Bajamonte's armed insurrection, it is said, floundered when a woman – Giustina Rossi – dropped a mortar on to the head of his standard-bearer in the street below, killing him instantly and stopping the rebels in their tracks.

Like the Gracchi before him, Bajamonte failed. His revolt is little more than a footnote in history, having done nothing to arrest the emergence within Venice of a rentier economy.* Perhaps that was the moment when the Republic started to die, in spirit if not yet in substance. Far from being the Republic's saviour, Bajamonte died in obscurity and has remained there ever since.

Venice's most famous son is instead a close contemporary of Bajamonte's – Marco Polo. He became famous not for insurrection but for exploration. Polo's travels revealed, even if at times they exaggerated, that progress was not just something that happened in the Mediterranean. China was in many ways at that time far advanced compared to much of Europe, including even Venice.

---

* An interesting footnote to this footnote; Giustina Rossi's reward for stopping the rebels and thereby saving a republic of rent seekers was, appropriately, to be permitted to live on a fixed low rent in her apartment for the rest of her days.

PART III

ARRESTED DEVELOPMENT

8

CHINA STALLED

The rise of contemporary China is one of the most striking, and epoch-defining developments of our age. A country that could barely feed herself within living memory, is poised to become *the* global economic super power. China has gone from being an agricultural economy, with a per-capita output little different to what it was two thousand years ago, to being an advanced digital economy within the space of sixty years.

China's economic output exceeded Britain's in the late 1990s. She leapfrogged Germany in the early twenty-first century, and Japan by 2011. By 2017, China's total GDP of US$11.2 trillion was second only to that of the United States, with its annual output of US$18 trillion. Yet with a growth rate over three times faster than America's, China seems set to surpass even America by 2030.

According to some estimates, China's economy is likely to be some 40 per cent larger than the US economy within two decades.

We are seeing a dramatic shift in the global balance of power. But if you take a slightly longer view of things, what we are actually witnessing is a reversion to the way things were for most of the past two or three millennia.

PRECOCIOUS PROMISE

Ever since the Neolithic revolution, China – with a large slice of the world's farmland and farmers – has been the most populous place on the planet, accounting fairly consistently for most of that time for a large slice of world economic output. As a rough rule of thumb, China routinely accounted for about a quarter of world economic output between AD 1 and 1500, with roughly twice as many people living there as in Europe since the fall of the Roman Empire. While Europe regressed after the fall of the Roman Empire, China saw gradual growth in per-capita output.

'Of all the civilizations of pre-modern times,' wrote the historian Paul Kennedy, 'none appeared more advanced, none felt more superior, than that of China.'* China's

* Kennedy, P., *The Rise and Fall of the Great Powers* (1987), p. 4.

fertile river valleys were highly productive. Advances in agriculture under the Song dynasty (960–1279) saw the development of wet-rice cultivation, which opened up parts of southern China to farming. Chinese cities dwarfed any of the urban settlements found in Europe at the time. She had an extensive canal system, which opened her up to the possibility of internal trade and travel. For much of the past two thousand years, China was politically unified and administered by a sophisticated bureaucracy.

In terms of innovation, China has been at the forefront of technological progress, too. China invented printing by the ninth century, building up large libraries. Gunpowder was being used by the eleventh century. The wheelbarrow, stirrup, compass, paper, porcelain and silk are all Chinese innovations. When Venice's most famous son, Marco Polo, visited China in the late thirteenth century, she was in some ways more technologically sophisticated than Europe's most advanced state at the time.

Medieval China had invented water-powered machines to spin hemp – something England's Arkwright was not to emulate for half a millennium. China operated enormous blast furnaces, producing vast quantities of iron. By the end of the eleventh century, according to Kennedy, Chinese iron output was 125,000 tons a year, a figure not exceeded by Britain until her Industrial Revolution seven centuries later.

China had, in the words of the historian David Landes,

'almost every element usually regarded by historians as a major contributory cause of the industrial revolution in north western Europe'. China not only had what many regard as the key ingredients, she had them centuries before Europe. And yet take-off never quite materialized.

No matter how much Marco Polo might have marvelled at the wealth he found in the imperial courts of the Far East, in per-capita terms, Chinese output per person had hardly increased at all in over a thousand years. Even in 1500, when per-capita output in Italy was roughly back to where it had been in Roman times, it was hardly higher than subsistence level in China.

In fact, in all sorts of ways, not long after Marco Polo's visit, China seems to have gone into reverse. Per-capita output peaked under the Song in the tenth and eleventh centuries, and then fell, not only when compared to Italy but in absolute terms. By the sixteenth century, China was probably poorer than she had been in the eleventh century.

Why? Because for all her early gains, the parasitic in China smothered the productive.

DYNASTIES OF DESTRUCTION

It was, according to certain contemporary Chinese academics, all the fault of the Qing.

Everything in China was going rather well, they

suggest, until these Manchurian interlopers showed up and established their own dynasty.

If this 'Qing conquest theory' is to be believed, one bad dynasty ruling over China between 1644 and 1911 accounts for the great divergence between China and Europe.

It's easy to see why some might find this account appealing. For a start, it fits a nationalist narrative – foreigners from Manchuria are to blame. And if the Qing are painted to be uniquely bad, does that not reinforce the credentials of China's current Communist Party, who can claim to have tidied things up after the Qing and the chaos that followed?

And perhaps there is something in this theory. Qing emperors did indeed make a succession of catastrophic choices. They presided over a parasitic state that weakened the productive and put China ever further behind the West.

But one thing that the 'Qing conquest theory' overlooks is that the Qing were not a uniquely disastrous dynasty. China had started to stall long before the Qing took over in the seventeenth century.

If one wants to point the finger at a dynasty of destructive outsiders, one should perhaps start with Kublai Khan, grandson of Genghis, who conquered China in 1279. This Mongol invasion brought death and destruction to China on an epic scale. Output fell from the peak it had achieved under the Song. By 1290, a decade or so after the conquest, there are reports of large number of commoners selling their children into slavery to meet the extortionate tax demands of this elite.

The ruling Yuan dynasty (1279–1368) that lived off the harvest of Han Chinese farmers might have been Mongolian, rather than Chinese, in origin, but China has proved perfectly capable of producing her own home-grown parasites.

When the Mongolian overlords were eventually driven out, the ethnically Chinese Ming dynasty (1363–1644) proved equally overbearing. Yuan, Ming or Qing, each of these different dynasties tended to preside over China in a similar style. The ethnicity of the emperor might have varied, but the machinery of the Chinese state that sustained them remained in many respects the same.

A vast hierarchy of officials raised taxes, issued orders and orchestrated official business. Tens of thousands of scholar-officials and lesser functionaries, each entitled to live off the proceeds of farmers, held sway.

Individual emperors and dynasties might have come and gone, but except for the occasional brief, often bloody, interlude, the mandarinate remained the same. And it was this mandarinate, more than any particular dynasty, that parasitized off the productive.

They sought monopolies consistently down the centuries to ensure officials were able to reap the proceeds of production. Officials set the price of commodities. Merchants were registered and taxed. Peasant farmers were heavily taxed to the point of subsistence existence. Any surplus was taken by the ruling elite.

Almost all areas of economic life were controlled by the mandarinate. Under the Ming, wrote French sinologist Étienne Balázs, 'no private undertakings nor any aspect of public life could escape official regulation…' There were 'clothing regulations, a regulation of public and private construction (dimension of houses)… all regulated'. There were state monopolies on salt, iron, tea, education and the use of the printed word.

China might have famously invented silk, and it was from its role in carrying this precious cargo that the Silk Road – that elongated trade route that runs between East and West – gets its name. But for most of the past millennium the production of silk in China was controlled by the state, with each household expected to pay a silk tax.

China was able to produce a water-powered textile machine in the fourteenth century, but she never produced a Richard Arkwright, whose water frame powered England's early industrial take-off. The compass guided not Chinese ships into European ports, but Portuguese and Spanish vessels on great voyages of global discovery.

China achieved a precocious style and standard of porcelain production in the sixteenth century, but she never managed the kind of mass production of what

Europeans called 'China' that Josiah Wedgwood achieved in the eighteenth century. Paper and printing might have been Chinese inventions, but there were precious few new publications produced in China to add to the sum of secular knowledge.

China might have had a unified, hierarchical administration run by a well-educated Confucian bureaucracy, but they did not preside over progress. On the contrary, China failed precisely because she was presided over by these surplus-sucking, innovation-stifling parasites.

The Chinese mandarin state expropriated and oversaw, regulated and repressed. It took over any activity seen to be lucrative, prohibited what it could not control, fixed prices and extracted bribes. A class of omnipotent bureaucrats produced rules to govern every aspect of commerce, trade, production and indeed life itself, from the cradle to the grave.

Under the Song, there had been a market economy in rural areas, with millions of tenant farmers. Under the Yuan, Ming and the Qing they became hereditary serfs. Both the Ming and the Qing banned overseas trade. In 1432, an imperial edict proscribed the construction of ocean-going ships. Between 1644 and 1683, the ban in foreign trade was made total. After then, it could only be conducted through a single port, Guangzhou. Trade, when allowed, had to be conducted through guilds, which were prohibited from competing with one another.

China's mandarinate not only closed her off to trade, but to new ideas. Scholars were persecuted for failing to stick to the approved scripts. China became a 'culturally and intellectually homeostatic society'.*

By the end of the nineteenth century, China's population of 400 million was toiling to support a parasitic elite of 7.5 million, or 2 per cent of the population, who consumed almost a quarter of total national product. Despite all the initial promise, parasitism prevented China from taking off. In the mid-twentieth century, China was as poor and underdeveloped as she had been a thousand years before.

The idea that China only started to stall in the seventeenth century is perhaps attractive for contemporary commentators wanting to believe that somehow the loss of momentum was only momentary. But the evidence suggests otherwise. China had started to diverge from Europe much earlier than those who blame it all on the Qing allow for. Eleventh-century China under the Song rulers was a richer place than Domesday England under the Normans. Yet by the time Emperor Hongwu founded the Ming dynasty in the late fourteenth century, England's per-capita output had already overtaken China's.

---

* Landes, D., *The Wealth and Poverty of Nations: Why Some Are So Rich and Some So Poor* (1998), p. 33.

Precisely which set of parasites should shoulder the blame for China's ruin is open to debate. That they ruined her is not.

After the Communists declared victory in 1949, China might have been free from predatory outsiders but for the next thirty years she was at the mercy of internal autocrats or worse. Attempts to order Chinese society by top-down design – Great Leaps Forward – and then, of course, via the Cultural Revolution, caused famine and catastrophe. It was not until the late 1970s that China's potential – so long enormous – started to be realized.

9

STASIS IN THE MIDDLE EAST AND INDIA

Imagine that there had been an intergalactic traveller whizzing through our solar system a thousand years ago. What do you suppose they might have made of our blue planet as they caught a glimpse of it far below?

Humans, they might have observed, were well-established and – with the exception of a few places like New Zealand – had spread across pretty much every habitable corner of the planet. But overwhelmingly, they might also have noticed, humans lived in Asia. It is estimated that in AD 1000, about seven out of every ten people lived in Asia.

If our space visitor took a bit more trouble to understand what these earthlings were up to, they might also have noticed that most human economic activity happened in Asia, too. Over in east Asia, China showed precocious signs of promise. But so, too, did some societies in southern and western Asia.

However much our space explorer might have looked elsewhere, there would have been few signs of more than rudimentary progress. Rome by then was a forgotten memory. Had they gazed at northern Europe, they would have seen little more than thick forests, peasant hovels and the occasional church or castle. Much of Africa, Oceania and the Americas would have seemed pretty empty of people – there just were not many living there. It is what was happening in China, and after that India and the Middle East, that would have caught any outside observer's attention.

THE ABBASID EMPIRE

Early Islam's capacity for wealth creation was considerable. Carved out of the wreckage of the eastern half of the Roman Empire, the Abbasid overlords extended their rule dramatically, and as they did so, their rule conferred on the conquered territories many of the conditions needed to induce intensive economic growth.

The Middle East achieved a brief period of such growth and innovation, and the Arabs under the early Abbasids grew rich through production, not plunder. In everything from mathematics and map-making to medicine and mill technology, the Muslim world led the way. By AD 1000, Abbasid Baghdad was one of the richest places on earth. Per-capita GDP reached US$650 per year in today's money – substantially above the measly US$427 in Europe at the same time.

The Abbasid Empire formed what was, in effect, a giant single market. Within it, there was something of an agricultural revolution between AD 700 and AD 1100, with big advances in irrigation and the adoption of new crops, such as sugar, rice and cotton. Early Islam encouraged enterprise and free markets. While European rulers and pontiffs in the early Middle Ages were in the business of decreeing what constituted a 'fair' price, Muhammad – himself once a merchant – had declared prices to be 'in the hands of God'. It's no coincidence that many of the words we use today when we talk about trade – tariff, check, carat – are Arab in origin.

Under the early Abbasids, the Middle East enjoyed a new monetary regime and a legal system that allowed trade centres – *funquqs* – charitable trusts – *waqfs* – and an Arab version of the later Venetian *commenda* contract – *qirad* – which allowed capital to be invested in trading ventures with liability limited. In fact, the historian of early Islam, Benedikt Koehler, argues that it was the other way round; the *commenda* was really a Venetian version of the *qirad* contract. The Venetians, he shows, got their idea for *commenda* contracts from the Arabs. Capitalism in northern Italy, he goes on to suggest, or rather the institutional arrangements and legal ideas that made it possible, did not arise in a vacuum. These ideas, rather like the new system of what we mistakenly sometimes refer to as 'Arabic' numerals, that were slowly taking hold in Europe came via the Muslim world.

It is certainly the case that the Arab *qirad* and the Venetian *commenda* contracts were – like the Roman system of bottomry loans before them – a strikingly similar answer to the problem of how to ensure capital could be invested, risks managed and liabilities limited. Whether each approach arose independently of one another or whether the Venetians were emulating the Arabs with whom they traded in the East, the more important point surely is that such arrangements – be it bottomry, *qirad* or *commenda* contracts – could only have arisen in a society where the rights of the productive were relatively secure.

These conditions, so favourable to the productive interest, did not last. From the tenth and eleventh centuries on, the elites started to extort. Perhaps the first big change came when the Abbasids stopped using a land tax to generate revenue, which meant that liabilities were relatively immune from any arbitrary system of collection. Instead they moved to a system of tax-farming, auctioning the right to collect taxes. This encouraged tax-collectors to extract whatever wealth they could from a province as quickly as they could, with little regard to future output. From there, the Abbasid elite moved on to doing what the Roman elite had resorted to – the straightforward expropriation of property.

The Abbasid Empire became just another extortion racket. Innovation stopped. Per-capita output fell. Egypt, under the successor regime of the Ayyubids, moved from tax-farming to feudalism – with military service expected in place of set taxes. This suggests that farmers were not producing much of a surplus that could be extorted at all, and so they were paying instead with direct service. After 1171, trade became overtly protectionist.

In 1258, Baghdad was sacked by a Mongol army. Her libraries were burnt, her population killed, and she was left as little more than a ruin. This calamity marked the end of a golden age for Baghdad. But for all the riches that the Abbasid elite had accumulated, the per-capita income of the Abbasid Empire on the eve of Baghdad's destruction was back to the level it had been two-and-a-half centuries before. Decline had arrived long before Hulagu Khan's army turned up. Like Rome almost a millennium before, the barbarian hordes fought to carve up a corpse.

If in the tenth century, the world's leading scientists might have written in Arabic, they did little thereafter to enhance technology in the Muslim world. The Muslim world began to regress to an almost European level of backwardness. By 1429, the Mamluk regime in Egypt, which maintained power through a slave army, was debasing the currency and banning exports of certain commodities altogether. For all the promise of progress in the early days of Islam, for most of the Middle Ages it was parasitism that actually prevailed.

OTTOMAN TURKS

A nomadic tribe that emerged out of central Asia in the seventh and eight centuries, the Turks converted to Islam along the way. In 1071 they won a great victory over Byzantium at the battle of Manzikert, marking the moment that they started to overwhelm what was left of the Eastern Roman Empire. It took them almost four hundred years to finish the job, but eventually, in 1453, they captured Constantinople.

From there they began to overrun the Venetian empire in the eastern Mediterranean. Then Syria and Egypt. They went on to conquer most of the Middle East, ruling a domain that stretched from Mesopotamia to Hungary.

By the time of Suleiman I, this Ottoman Empire had around 14 million subjects and was perhaps the most formidable military machine on the planet. But the Ottoman Empire was a plunder machine, better at accumulating wealth than generating it. It was fuelled, rather like a supernova star, by sucking in material from outside to keep it going. And like a supernova, once it had run out of external fuel, it started to eat itself.

Overstretched by the mid-sixteenth century, the Ottoman armies could no longer conquer others. So the elite soldiers, the Janissaries, plundered their own domains with evermore intensity.

From 1556, a succession of sultans ruled the Empire with more interest in enjoying the proceeds of plunder than in much else. To keep tax revenues flowing, taxes were imposed on trade, and goods and property were confiscated. Tax farmers were unleashed to prey upon the peasants, scouring the land for signs of any surplus that they could extract. Taxes became so extortionate that Ottoman rule began to actually depopulate large swathes of territory.

It is estimated that during the reign of the sixteenth-century sultan Suleiman the Magnificent, the fifty highest-ranking Ottoman officials received 15 per cent of total expenditure. These are some of the most extreme instances of wealth inequality anywhere in human history – and it certainly was not a surfeit of capitalism that was to blame.

About the only road open to personal enrichment within the Ottoman Empire by the sixteenth century lay in purchasing a public post – and using it to extort.

Trade depended on concessions granted by the authorities. Exports were prohibited, and imports permitted only if they served the interests of the elite. So concerned were the rulers to maintain their hold that they tried to keep outside influences at bay, going so far as to ban the printing press entirely.

By 1600 output and incomes per capita in those parts of the Middle East ruled by the Ottomans were below what they had been under Roman rule a millennium and a half earlier.

INDIA

Historians often like to attribute underdevelopment in certain societies to some sort of outside agency. For some Chinese historians, it was the arrival of foreigners, the Qing, which accounted for China's backwardness from the seventeenth century. If the Qing conquest theory is used to explain Chinese underdevelopment, something similar – call it British conquest theory – is used by some to explain India's underdevelopment.

According to this school of thought, India in the eighteenth century, just like China before it, was poised to take off. Until a group of outsiders – from England, rather than Manchuria – turned up, plunging the country backwards.

Perhaps India was poised to take off before the British arrived. But the trouble with blaming India's under-development on the British is that they were just the latest in a long succession of invaders. Before the British came by sea, Persians and Parthians, the Mughals and Tamerlane, and even Arabs, Greeks and Scythians, had all come by land over the mountains of Afghanistan.

For much of her history, India has been ruled by a succession of outside parasites. At about the same time that the Ottomans were extending their grip into Europe, another Muslim army invaded India. Babar, the king of Kabul, established Mughal rule in India from 1526. While his hold was shaky to start with, Mughal rule was consolidated by his grandson, Akbar (1556–1605), who extended the Mughal Empire further south.

The Mughal elite, rather like the Ottomans, ruled over a mass of (mainly Hindu) farmers. Like the Ottomans, they lived off the proceeds of taxes and tolls, and had little involvement in any kind of productive activity. Surrounded by slaves, servants and splendour, they luxuriated in water gardens, milking rural India for what they could extract.

Lesser nobles were subject to 100 per cent death duties, their estates becoming the personal property of the emperor on their death. Jagir estates were a form of feudal land grant, gifted by the emperor to his underlings. Yet they remained the personal property of the emperor, and could be taken away from the cronies he gifted them to at any time. This, of course, encouraged whoever happened to be in possession of them at any one time to make the most of them, and extract what they could from the peasant farmers that they found there as quickly as they could.

The effect was catastrophic in terms of inhibiting agricultural output. According to the French physician François Bernier, who lived at the court of the seventeenth-century Mughal Emperor Aurangzeb, property rights were so insecure that nominal land owners would not so much as bother to clear a ditch or repair a house for fear it would be confiscated.

Like the Romans, the Mughals debased the coinage as a means of extortion. Trade monopolies were awarded in return for bribes. At the time of Emperor Akbar's death in 1605, three-quarters of the land tax, approximately two-thirds of total revenue, went to the army – and that was long after Akbar had stopped waging external wars. The emperor and his top 122 officials received about one-eighth of national product. That is to say, 0.0006 per cent of households took 12.5 per cent of total wealth.

There was almost no innovation in northern India under the Mughals. Indeed, it was not until the nineteenth century that Gutenberg's idea of a printing press came to India. The colossal mass of ordinary Indians existed in a state of crushing poverty. Parasitism induced sclerosis.

Per-capita output remained unchanged for a century and a half after Akbar – before falling further in the late eighteenth century.

However vast India was in terms of population and the output that the peasantry produced, for much of her history she never rose above a subsistence level of output. And this was not just due to the various external elites that ruled over her. The parasitic system that kept India underdeveloped was not due simply to outsiders. It was internalized as the caste system, and deeply embedded within Indian society.

Based on Hindu scripture, India's caste system has ordered society across the Subcontinent for much of recorded history. The caste system made membership of guilds hereditary. Only those born to produce and sell certain things could do so. As was so often the case, traders and merchants – the Vaisya – were pretty close to the bottom of the pecking order. And it was this caste system – with hereditary positions and rigid labour rules – as much as any external overlords that helped hinder India's development.

Like Europe, India in the Middle Ages consisted of a mosaic of competing kingdoms and empires. The fortunes of the rulers and their ruling dynasties might have waxed and waned, but society across much of India was hierarchical, and divided up into sharply defined castes.

Perhaps one of the reasons why invaders had found

it possible to subjugate India in the first place was the existence of this Hindu hierarchy. When the Mughal over-ran India, they grafted themselves on as a new ruling elite. The British did something rather similar. In both in-stances, the caste system that underpinned Indian society remained largely unchanged.

However much the Mughals or the East India Company might have extorted India, India had her own home-grown parasitic system. India was locked in a Malthusian trap of her own making long before either the British or the Mughal arrived.

10

SLOW ADVANCE –
THE MIDDLE AGES

If China, the Middle East and India were inhibited by elites, with signs of early promise snuffed out, they at least never managed to regress quite as far and as dramatically as Western Europe did between the fifth and tenth centuries.

Predation and parasitism destroyed civilization across Europe. For almost a thousand years, Europe was in a period we call the Dark Ages. We know so little about it because literate society had ceased to exist apart from in a few pockets. Only very slowly did Europe – or at least, some parts of it – begin to emerge out of this epoch of backwardness. One of the first places to start to show some signs of progress was northern Italy.

NORTHERN ITALY

It was not just Venice that started to show signs of progress in the early Middle Ages. A number of other city-states – notably Milan, Florence, Cremona, Pisa and Genoa – began to acquire some of the pre-conditions for progress: independence – as the power of the emperor over city-states waned; dispersed power – as the communes adopted republican constitutions; and interdependence – as trade picked up.

The manorial system that had started to take shape in the century before the collapse of Roman authority in Western Europe, began to disintegrate in northern Italy in the mid-twelfth century. This hints at the end of complete self-sufficiency, with greater monetary trade and therefore more specialization and exchange – and wealth.

Italy also started to see innovation, with the invention, for example, of the mechanical clock and spectacles, as well as improvements in the design of ships, artillery and windmills. There was, at the same time, financial innovation, with the advent of bills of exchange and banking allowing greater trade. Medieval Italy experienced a marked increase in consumption and productive investment, too. The Italian economic historian Carlo Cipolla recounts how, in the eleventh century, the opening of a new mill was a major deal in the neighbourhood. A couple of centuries later, mills were commonplace.*

Markets and regional trade fairs also expanded across much of Europe. There was a massive expansion in textile processing before 1350, using imported cotton, silk and know-how from the East. Lucca had water-powered silk works by 1200. In Milan, there were an estimated six to nine thousand cotton workers by 1348, and even more in Florence and Genoa.

It seemed that northern Italy in the twelfth and thirteenth centuries was on the verge of the kind of textile revolution that England underwent 500 years later. But it never happened. The pull of the parasites was just too strong. Take-off stalled – just as it did in China and elsewhere.

During the fourteenth century, to an even greater extent than happened in Venice, power in the other northern Italian city-states was concentrated in the hands of a few. Consuls, who had administered many city-states in the communes' republican tradition, were replaced by *podestà* magistrates, whose positions often became hereditary. While Venice moved from an open to a closed system of oligarchy, most other Italian city-states ended up in the hands of a tyrant, or *il signore*.

---

* Cipolla, C., *Before the Industrial Revolution: European Society and Economy 1000–1700* (1993), p. 219.

Perhaps what made Venice exceptional is that she was able to stave off the parasites a little more effectively and for a little longer than many of the other city-states around her.

The *signore* elites that emerged in most medieval Italian city-states found it easier to enrich themselves through taxation than via the difficult business of commerce. Tax revenues in city-states increased dramatically as the princelings milked the merchants. Annual expenditure in Siena, for example, rose from a modest 6,300 lira in 1226 to a crushing 347,000 lira by 1328. This was a massive addition to the burden that the *signori* imposed on merchants and the productive. In addition, forced loans were not uncommon A wealthy merchant would find himself becoming the owner of a virtually worthless IOU, in return for lending the civic authorities a large sum of ready cash.

Taxes were then spent in ways that rewarded parasites: interest payments on loans – so bondholders did well; increased military spending – so mercenaries, or *condotti*, did well. In Venice, defence expenditure meant generous contracts awarded to vested interests not especially good at converting financial strength into naval muscle – so suppliers might have done well, too.

The emergence of parasitic *signori* allowed a tiny elite to accumulate capital in the Italian cities. In 1427, for example, the richest 10 per cent in Florence had 68 per cent of the wealth; the poorest 60 per cent, a mere 5 per cent.*

The *signori* were not the only parasites in the communes. As in Venice, guilds restricted free exchange as well. They compelled producers to use established techniques, impeding innovation. They set quality standards, preventing producers from supplying lower-cost products to a potentially wider market. They made sure only certain kinds of apprentices could make particular sorts of products, or work in certain trades. They even had the right to seize the goods of any rivals threatening to offer the customer a better deal.

So, as happened in Venice, textile exports across northern Italy collapsed. The proto-industrialization that seemed to be gaining momentum in northern Italian cities fizzled out. In the early 1500s, the number of woollen workshops in Florence fell from 270 to 60. Its nascent industry lost market share to Dutch and English competitors unhindered by anti-competitive practices.

Having been at the forefront of economic development and innovation in Europe between 1000 and 1500, Italy stagnated. Per-capita output in Italy had increased to around US$2,000 (in 1990 prices), well over subsistence levels, by the early fifteenth century. By 1500, per-capita output had fallen back and kept falling. By 1600

* Ibid., p. 11.

Italy was poorer than she had been a century and a half before.

We must add northern Italy to that long list of places – including China under the Yuan, Ming and Qing, the Middle East under the Abbasids, and India under the Mughals – where even the most promising progress came to grief as a consequence of small parasitic elites.

GRINDINGLY SLOW ESCAPE

Historians of the Middle Ages seem to report finding a 'renaissance' wherever they look. Some have claimed to have spotted a Carolingian renaissance in the eighth and ninth centuries. Others say they found one in the tenth century, while several medieval renaissances are alleged to have happened in the twelfth century. Perhaps these discoveries tell us more about the tendency specialist historians have to overstate the significance of 'their' period of history than they do about the past.

During the Middle Ages, some progress took place. There were improvements in farming, with the adoption of a heavier, wheeled plough and the use of crop rotation. Milling technology improved, with more water mills and new designs of windmill. But the Middle Ages need to be put into perspective. Between 1000 and 1500, per-capita output in the West rose from US$426 to US$754 in today's money. Or by 77 per cent stretched out over half a millennium.

It was grindingly, painfully slow. We have experienced more economic expansion in the past three decades than there was in half a millennium during the Middle Ages. Indeed, growth in the Middle Ages wasn't just slow from a modern perspective but by the standards of the Roman Republic. Per-capita output in Italy doubled over a period of 300 years between 300 BC and AD 14 – more than the increase in output over 500 years in the Middle Ages.

By 1500, Europe might have progressed in relation to other parts of the world but it was by no means clear that she was ahead – certainly not militarily. She endured a series of military defeats: Wahlstatt in 1241, Nicopolis in 1396 and the Siege of Vienna in 1529 – following which the Balkans were lost to the Ottomans.

E. L. Jones, the famous Australian scholar, wrote about the 'European miracle'. But before the sixteenth century, if not the nineteenth for many, it was an extraordinarily slow-moving miracle. In fact, progress was so slow during the Middle Ages that, after 500 years of successive renaissances, Europe's per-capita output was still below what it had been in Italy in the first century AD.

Europe had not made enough progress between the tenth and fourteenth centuries to escape Malthusian constraints. The Black Death in the mid-fourteenth century was a brutal manifestation of this fact. From 1348 to the 1650s, a series of catastrophic plagues reduced Europe's population by between a quarter and a third. War and famine played their part, too. In 1500, Europe's population of 60 to 70 million was lower than its estimated 80 million in 1300. For all the progress of the Middle Ages, there was no miraculous escape from age-old constraints.

But, despite this, Europe in the Middle Ages was one of the few places on the planet where there had been any intensive economic growth over the preceding two millennia. Why was it that Europe made progress, albeit so slowly? Because she was steadily starting to escape the grip of the parasites.

If you study a map of Europe in 1500, you will see it consisted of a mosaic of states and statelets. In contrast to China, or the empires of the Mughals, Abbasids or Ottomans, Europe was never unified politically.

'There existed no uniform authority in Europe which could effectively halt this or that commercial development,' writes Paul Kennedy. 'No central government whose changes in priorities could cause the rise and fall of a particular industry; no systematic and universal plundering of businessmen and entrepreneurs by tax gatherers, which so retarded the economy of Mogul India.'*

* Kennedy, P., *The Rise and Fall of the Great Powers* (1987), p. 19.

The closest thing to any kind of pan-European authority, the papacy, was weak. As we have seen, Venice could simply ignore the papal ban on overseas trading with Muslims in a way that Chinese traders couldn't ignore similar bans under the Ming. Without a single political authority imposing uniform policy, there could be – to use modern management-speak – systems competition, like there was in ancient Greece.

If one prince taxed trade too highly, or imposed too many obligations on merchants, they would move. If one king repudiated his debts, he would find it hard to get a loan again. Good ideas and innovation could spread. Semi-autonomous cities in the Middle Ages were a distinctively European phenomenon. There were no equivalents to Dutch burghers or Italian communes in Japan, India or China, beyond the jurisdiction of the emperor or local warlord.

Harvard economist and historian David Landes, author of *The Wealth and Poverty of Nations*, recounts the story of how the Count of Flanders in the twelfth century marched into Bruges to reclaim a runaway serf. The townsfolk drove him and his henchmen out. Fragmentation did not prevent parasitism but it was a restraining influence. During the Middle Ages, it is possible to see, very gradually, the slow emergence of a market economy, greater respect for property rights and the restraining influence of the law.

There was a gradual 'widening of the market that promoted specialization and division of labour', according to Landes. And it meant that 'the world of Adam Smith was already taking shape 500 years before his time'.*

Painfully slowly the hold of the parasites seemed to be waning. Why has their hold proved so strong and resilient?

* Landes, D., *The Wealth and Poverty of Nations: Why Some Are So Rich and Some So Poor* (1998), p. 44.

11

WHY PARASITES PREVAIL

Often elites have relied on sheer brute force. The Yuan rulers of China, or the Normans in England, would maintain garrisons across the country to ensure taxes were collected, and their will prevailed. From the time of Norman rule over England to Englishmen ruling over India, there have been endless examples of small elites maintaining their position over others through military might.

Force, however, is not enough to explain the ability of small elites to extort.

THE ROLE OF INSTITUTIONS

In *Why Nations Fail*, the economist Daron Acemoğlu and political scientist James Robinson make a compelling case to show how powerful elites are able to rig things through institutions. Drawing on the history of societies from central America in the sixteenth century to central Africa today, they argue that when a society's institutions are 'extractive' – operating in the interests of a parasitic few – societies remain in a state of Malthusian misery. It is, they suggest, only when institutions are 'inclusive' – and the surplus can no longer be siphoned off – that intensive growth is possible.

In Venice, they observe, the closure of the Great Council (the *Serrata*) and the subsequent creation of the Council of Ten served as a sort of institutional tipping-point – the moment when a relatively open Venetian oligarchy became increasingly exclusive and extractive. Going back even further, there was a shift in Rome away from a Senate and powerful elected magistrates towards a system of centralized, all-powerful emperors.

Extractive institutions, they point out, were not just the instruments of extortion. The shape of a society's institutions, they argue, determined if elites were extractive or not. Institutional determinism, however, puts the cart before the horse. Rome was long an oligarchy but power within the Roman Republic was not concentrated because the Senate overturned the position of the elected tribunes and the Tribal Assembly. The tribunes and Assembly lost their powers to the Senate because an evermore powerful elite had emerged there. Institutional change reflected the fact that there had been a shift in the balance of power within the Roman body politic, rather than causing it.

In late-thirteenth-century Venice, power was not concentrated because of the creation of extractive institutions. The new Council of Ten marked a concentration of power that had already happened – and which merely began to manifest itself in such institutional arrangements.

Perhaps the even bigger problem with institutional explanations as to why elites were able to extort is that it simply kicks the analytical can further down the road. If it's the shape of institutions that determine if a society takes off, what then determines if institutions are inclusive or extractive?

Acemoğlu and Robinson imply that good, inclusive institutions arose by accident. Extractive institutions get replaced by better, inclusive ones because of 'critical junctures' in history, they say. Inclusive institutions arise when 'propitious existing institutions' are already in place, they claim. And 'some luck' they suggest 'is key, because history always unfolds in a contingent way'.

Critical junctures? Propitious institutions already existing? Luck? Having advanced the idea that institutions were the primary causation when it comes to human progress, at the last moment Acemoğlu and Robinson veer back towards random determinism. Institutional determinism leaves us with the unsatisfactory idea that random chance shaped institutions.

The prevalence of extractive institutions in a particular society can help us understand how elites within a society entrench themselves. It does not necessarily account for why they should do so. So why was it that minority elites were able to maintain their hold on everyone else over the centuries?

Such arrangements would have seemed normal for most of human history, not only because that was just the way things were, but because of ethical systems that implied it was how things were supposed to be.

DENIGRATING THE PRODUCTIVE

Who do you most admire? Steve Jobs, the driving force behind one of the world's largest companies? Or Jack Ma, founder of Ali Baba, the greatest retail business on the planet? Or Ma Huateng, who has amassed an even greater fortune? Or maybe Mark Zuckerberg, a zillionaire before he turned thirty? What about Elon Musk, with his remarkable vision of hyperloops and reusable space rockets – and the occasional eccentric tweet? Or the guy at the end of the street where you live who has just opened a new artisanal bakery?

In productive societies, the productive tend to be

admired and well treated. Today we – albeit at times grudgingly – respect entrepreneurs, even Mark Zuckerberg and Elon Musk. So, too, in early-Republican Rome, the self-made men and merchants – the *equites* class – were respected. They shared the Senate with patricians as equals.

Likewise, in the early-medieval period Venice was a city of merchants, run by and for the merchant interest. So, too, in many northern Italian city-states before 1350, and in the towns and cities of Flanders in the seventeenth century. Traders and middlemen were free to live under merchant-made laws and were not beholden to the whims of kings or the extortion of emperors.

In Britain, the city fathers who built Glasgow and Birmingham during the nineteenth century at a time of industrial take-off were merchants and businessmen. The city halls they erected were temples to trade; the exquisite details that decorated them, a celebration of commerce. Contrast that to the way that merchants and middlemen were treated in most pre-industrial societies.

American academic Deirdre McCloskey has noted how, in productive societies, merchants have been able to trade and exchange without being despised or persecuted. But in most pre-modern societies, she notes, 'the sneers of the aristocrats, the damning of the priest, the envy of the peasant, all directed against trade and profit... have long sufficed to kill economic growth'.*

Whether Edo Japan, medieval India or Ming China, each of these societies had one strikingly similar feature: rigidly hierarchical societies where merchants were always placed at the bottom of the pile.

In Japan, they were forced to live in their own urban quarters and without legal rights. In India, traders were lower caste. In China, merchants were made to wear distinctive clothes so as to stand out as objects of contempt. In 7 BC, Emperor Ai banned them from owning land or becoming a state official.

Merchants were endlessly told what prices they might charge, then were blamed for not supplying at the preferred price. They were taxed and regulated. They were ordered to extend credit and loans – and often found their debtors unilaterally cancelled the forced loan. After the *signori* took over the northern Italian city-states and started to prey on the productive, merchants began to be seen as menial and were excluded from the upper echelons of society.

In Rome in AD 301, at a time when the parasitic were firmly in the ascendency, Emperor Diocletian issued an edict that raged against merchants and middlemen for

---

* Deirdre McCloskey, 'Bourgeois Shakespeare Disdained Trade and the Bourgeoisie', talk given to the American Economic Association, 4 January 2015.

their 'unbridled passion for gain', threatening with the death penalty those who did not sell at the prices he preferred.

Merchants and middlemen were despised in medieval Europe and by the Ottoman elite. Ethnic groups associated with trade and exchange – Jews in fifteenth-century Spain, Asians in 1970s Uganda – were often demonized, persecuted and even driven out by the elites.

Elites no doubt found it easier to extort from those they first helped vilify. But in many pre-modern societies, it was not just a case of doing down the productive, or one particularly productive section of the population. Parasitic elites often promoted ethical codes that both legitimized the extortion of their hosts and encouraged the hosts' acquiescence.

PARASITE CREEDS

Think of those patrimonial societies which existed, often unchanged, for thousands of years in Egypt, Iraq, India and Mexico. They might have been separated by seas and centuries, but from the cities of the Aztecs to those of the Egyptians or Sumerians, these societies had some strikingly similar features: a small, powerful priesthood presiding over a mass of toiling farmers, aided by a caste of warriors.

Temples were often the political centres from which the state was administered. From pharaonic Egypt to ancient Mesopotamia, those that created the wealth – farmers and merchants – had their wealth taken from them in the name of a divinely ordained order. This sort of patrimonial parasitism was, if you like, sanctified. Peasants were expected to yield much of their harvest to their overlords, often leaving them little more than a subsistence existence.

Of course, force was available to ensure that the producers handed over their harvests. Non-payment of taxes was often regarded as insurrection and treated as such. Slavery or serfdom might have been the means of extortion, but such systems were not only underpinned by fear of the whip or worse. If slaves and serfs were never willing participants in the process of their own extortion, they were often – surprisingly, to our way of thinking – passive and pliant. There have been surprisingly few big slave revolts in recorded history; Spartacus' in the first century BC, the Zanj revolt in what we now call Iraq in the ninth century, and the slave rebellion in eighteenth-century French Haiti are rare examples.

Perhaps this reflects the fact that for long periods of time, those who laboured for their overlords were not only bound by whips and chains; they were bound by moral codes that inclined them to accept their servile status, perhaps in a way that we – with our twenty-first-century outlook – find hard to imagine. The priestly elites had implanted in the minds of their human hosts a bogus altruism, which demanded self-sacrifice in the interests of the divine – sometimes literally for the victims of the Aztec elite. In each of those ancient patrimonial societies, the creation myths might have differed but always the story contained the same constant: man was created to serve the gods – or at least their priestly representatives on earth.

The gods were lords, and the priests' and emperors' masters. Sin was defined as man seeking to live on his own terms – or, almost as bad, his failure to hand over half of the harvest.

Elites have constantly invoked a set of ethics that normalize extortion, legitimizing and sanctifying the transfer from the productive to the parasitic. The Abbasids and Ottomans invoked the Koran to justify a *djizya* tax on the unbelievers in order to pay for their life of luxury in their harems. The Christian church, too, invoked all manner of theological justification for leaving your estate to the church. When the Japanese peasants fed the *samurai* warrior caste, they did so because it was their divine duty to provide for them.

As the nineteenth-century French thinker Frederick Bastiat put it, 'When plunder becomes a way of life for a group of men living together in society, they create for themselves in the course of time a legal system that authorizes it and a moral code that glorifies it.'

The moral and legal codes prevalent in Confucian China, Brahmin India, Edo Japan and feudal Europe authorized and glorified extortion. Each of these codes was based on a bogus notion of reality, on superstition, custom and tradition. They elevated the interests of the parasitic over the productive.

Merchants in China were not at the bottom of the heap by accident. Confucian teaching deliberately and systematically placed them there. In an almost complete inversion of reality, merchants – the truly productive – were endlessly described as parasitic. Together with farmers, their role was to provide for the scholarly elite. Confucianism not only insisted on it, but insisted that it was celestially ordained.

After the expulsion of the Yuan dynasty, and in accordance with Confucian teachings, China's rulers encouraged self-sufficient farming communities. They deliberately discouraged trade not only with the outside world, but within China itself. Trade was repeatedly sanctioned as ignoble and unworthy. Had Jack Ma founded a trading company in fifteenth-century China, he would have been hounded by China's rulers, rather than feted as a national icon. If trade was to be tolerated, it was to be controlled and regulated.

Not only did these parasite creeds denigrate the productive and free exchange, they often sanctified their own extractive rule with self-reinforcing belief systems.

MIND CONTROL

For half of its life cycle, the parasitic lancet liver fluke lives inside a cow. For much of the other half, it lives in cow poo.

It's easy to work out how the fluke gets from its first home inside a cow to its second in a cow pat. But how does this tiny little parasitic worm manage to get back into the cow to complete its life cycle? It finds an unsuspecting host – an ant. And it gets inside its mind, literally.

The fluke infects the ant and then alters the neurochemistry of the ant's brain – particularly the part that controls locomotion. This causes the ant to climb to the top of a tall blade of grass, and stay there.

Why? So that the ant, atop the grass blade, gets eaten by a passing cow, allowing the fluke to get back to where it wants to be.

And it's not only liver flukes that alter the behaviour of their hosts in this way. Neuroparasitologists have discovered myriad ways in which parasitic organisms do not merely siphon resources off their host, but manipulate their minds to make them behave in ways that serve the parasite.

There is a species of hairworm that makes crickets and grasshoppers drown themselves in order to get into water, where they need to be to breed. A kind of wasp has been discovered that manipulates orb spiders to build them cocoons made of finest spider silk. When such parasites manipulate their hosts' behaviour, they do so by releasing neurochemicals into the host organism, which mimic the hosts' own neurochemistry. This isn't, of course, the only way that parasites manipulate their hosts' behaviour. Often, they do so by deceiving their hosts' sense of self-interest.

An adult warbler instinctively spends every daylight hour finding grubs to feed its fledglings. Its frantic feeding behaviour is intended to ensure its young grow as fast as possible, maximizing their chances of survival. But cuckoo chicks are, of course, masters at deception. Tricking the warbler into believing that it, the cuckoo chick, is part of its brood, it takes advantage of the warbler's feeding instinct, getting fed a steady supply of grubs – and killing off its smaller warbler step-siblings when Mum and Dad are not looking.

Perhaps human parasites are also in the business of manipulation and mind-control – not through neuro-chemistry but by deception? Do they not use an ethical sleight of hand to deceive their human hosts, making the population serve its own interests while believing they are acting in self-interest? More than that, surely extractive elites promulgate a deceptive image of reality to manipulate their hosts' behaviour to serve their own ends?

Perhaps this all sounds a little far-fetched? Isn't it all

just a little bit conspiratorial, these cunning elites con-
cocting fairy tales to deceive the masses?

How else do you account for the case of the Vaisya
caste living in India a thousand years ago? Farmers and
merchants, they produced the wealth yet paid extortionate taxes. Most of what the Vaisya produced they had to
hand over to the elite. The priestly Brahmin and warrior
Kshatriya castes, meanwhile, lived tax-free.

That was obviously unfair, right? Yes, to our twenty-
first-century way of thinking. But not if you bought into
the belief system of the time. Ancient Hindu ethics held
that the upper caste had belonged to a lower caste in a
previous life. It would be unjust, or so they argued, for
someone having paid high taxes in a former life to be
expected to pay them again in this one.

As for the lowly Vaisya, provided they paid their taxes
on time, they would be reborn into the upper castes in
the next life to enjoy their tax-free status then. Since they
would be tax exempt in the next life, was it not fair that
they pay them in this one?

Laughable? Absurd? Perhaps to our contemporary way
of thinking, but the way that people think can be manipulated. Our sense of right and wrong, what is fair and just,
are not constant but malleable. Many millions have lived
and died – and not just in medieval India – believing that
it was their lot in life to serve an elite – wittingly or otherwise – as part of some divinely sanctioned cosmic order.

Have you ever pondered why it was that in Europe in the Middle Ages, the Church became one of the largest landowners? Well, every farmer had to pay the Church one tenth of what they produced – the tithe. The proceeds of this tax were stored in the tithe barns, and if you didn't do your bit to keep the tithe barn stocked up, you would go to hell.

You and your children would go to hell too, if you didn't baptize them – and pay the Church as you did so. You'd go to hell if you didn't marry – and pay the Church for the privilege. You'd go to hell if you didn't pay to be buried on consecrated land. It's hardly surprising that the Church grew rich.

The Church also gained from grants of land from aristocrats, who in return had their offspring appointed to bishoprics and other powerful positions in the church. It was an exchange that suited both sides.

Long before Martin Luther protested the selling of indulgences, ecclesiastical ethics seemed to suit the material interests of the Church.

WHY DIDN'T PEOPLE WAKE UP?

'Surely people,' you might well wonder, 'would simply have seen the moral codes that aggrandized the priestly elites for what they were?' Luther no doubt felt the same.

How could people not see through the bogus conception of reality? Yet for generation after generation people didn't wake up to it.

For centuries in Europe, serfs submitted to their overlords and to knights. In Japan, the peasants did much the same to their *diamyo* and the *samurai*. Among the Maya, the lower orders – the *chembal uinieol* – sacrificed their harvests, and sometimes literally themselves, to the *almehenob* (princes) and the *ahkinob* (priests). Different cultures, different continents, but each time there was an ethical system, and a bogus notion of reality, to justify such submission. Like reed warbler parents, frantically feeding an oversized cuckoo chick, humans are often deluded into thinking that their interests are served by serving the parasites.

Perhaps it's hard to see what's happening because it's difficult to always discern what produces progress. Many ideas, like comparative advantage and specialization and exchange, are deeply counter-intuitive.

Societies in the hands of extractive, ruinous elites can appear successful and strong – at least for a while. Rome as an empire was greater and grander in almost every way than Rome as a mere republic had ever been. As an oligarchy sapped Italian society's productive strength, for several centuries Rome more than compensated for that by helping herself to the produce of others outside Italy.

The Roman elite amassed wealth by redistribution and, amidst the triumphs and imperial splendour, that aggrandizement would have seemed immediate and impressive. The decline of the underlying generator of this wealth – intensive economic growth through mutual exchange – was gradual and not immediately visible. Rome seemed more resplendent and imposing in AD 100 than she had in 100 BC. It would have been easy to believe that Roman exceptionalism lay in conquest and empire, rather than in a carefully devised republican tradition of dispersed power.

The Venetian state appeared at its most opulent and exuberant at a time of entrenched oligarchy. In fact, many of its greatest artistic and architectural achievements happened precisely because there was a wealthy, extravagant elite on hand to pour money on such things. Beneath the decadence and glitter, decline might have set in but it would not perhaps have been so apparent.

We don't even need to look back that far to see seeds of decline being mistaken for progress.

In 1980, Zimbabwe became an independent state. Far from thriving as a newly liberated democracy, she became Robert Mugabe's fiefdom, a sort of private kleptocracy. As a consequence, Zimbabwe's GDP per person fell by almost half between 1980 and 2010. Zimbabweans ate better on the day they achieved independence than they did thirty-three years later, when they had a lower daily calorie intake. Indeed, Zimbabwe is one of the few places on the planet that is poorer today than it was in the early 1980s.

But even despite such unequivocal decline, for many years both inside and outside Zimbabwe, Mugabe was lauded as a liberator by those who could not seem to see the destructive consequences of his government.

Imagine how much harder it must be to discern a more gradual decline, spread out over decades and generations. Or how difficult, bordering on the impossible, it would be to envisage not an actual loss of output, but a lost opportunity to have a higher output that never even materializes.

So long as parasites could propagate their bogus image of reality, their hold on society stayed strong – and there was little hope that humans could escape the Malthusian trap. Where parasites were weaker, progress was possible. 'Market activity was greatest in areas of half-hearted control such as borderlands between feudal units or pairs of political authorities.'* Or on inaccessible mud banks, such as Venice. Or in that other swampy corner of Europe, known as the Netherlands – home of the world's first industrial revolution.

* Jones, E., *The European Miracle: Environments, economies and geopolitics in the history of Europe and Asia* (1981), p. 91.

It was in such places, peripheral to not only European power politics but to the creeds of mind-control, that progress became possible.

PART IV

THE MIRACLE OF MODERNITY

12

DUTCH BOOM

The world's first industrial revolution didn't happen in England. It occurred on the other side of the North Sea, in Holland. Contrary to conventional wisdom, it was the Dutch that produced the world's first modern economy.

It was there in the sixteenth century, one hundred and fifty years before anything like it happened in England, that per-capita incomes started to increase from one decade to the next. This was something that few other societies had ever achieved before.

Previously, where riches had been amassed, it had been in the courts and harems of kings and emperors through redistribution. The wealth was taken from many and given to a few. Those that had above-average incomes acquired them by taking off everyone else. In the Netherlands from the sixteenth century, wealth came to be generated rather than simply gathered. How and why did this happen?

TAKE-OFF

By the early sixteenth century, output per person in the Netherlands was already as high as anywhere in Europe, with the possible exception of northern Italy. But then over three generations in the seventeenth century, Dutch per-capita output rose by a greater amount than had happened during all the previous generations who had ever lived anywhere. By the start of the eighteenth century, while almost 60 per cent of people in the UK were still engaged in agriculture, a mere 40 per cent of the Dutch still worked the land, with approximately a third of the workforce in industry.*

At first glance, Holland's emergence was unlikely. Like Venice, the Netherlands was a soggy backwater, with few natural resources. Yet like Venice, the Dutch had the

* For more detail about urbanization, and the transition from agriculture to industry, see Wrigley, A., 'Urban Growth and Agricultural Change: England and the Continent in the Early Modern Period', *The Journal of Interdisciplinary History* (1985), pp. 683–728.

key conditions that make intensive economic growth possible.

Firstly, the Dutch achieved their independence, ousting those archetypal parasites, the Habsburgs, during the Dutch Revolt that started in the 1560s. On several occasions, it looked as though the Dutch might get gobbled up, before the Habsburgs finally gave up trying to rule the Netherlands in 1648.

Secondly, power within the new Republic was dispersed. The Union of Utrecht in 1579 loosely amalgamated seven different Dutch provinces under a central administration. While a central authority, in the shape of a *Stadtholder* – or monarch – and the States General – or parliament – were to oversee a common defence, foreign and, to some extent, fiscal policy, the towns and provinces retained a great deal of autonomy.

The Dutch had long had a tradition of autonomy. At a very local level, the drainage boards, or *waterschappen* – important institutions in a country prone to flooding – possessed their own independent tax-raising powers. Long before the sixteenth century, feudalism – in the strict sense of the term – had disappeared among the Dutch. William the Silent, the leader of the Dutch revolt against Spain, observed in 1538 that 'there are no feudal goods in the countryside... for all the lands are freely owned'. Towns, too, had tended to govern their own affairs.

The new Republic had the third and final ingredient for economic take-off – she was interconnected and open to exchange. Sitting at a confluence of waterways, her merchants were able to trade upstream along the Rhine and into the European interior. The sea linked her to the Baltics and Scandinavia, England, France, Spain, the Mediterranean and beyond.

Dutch ocean-going *fluyt* ships opened up new markets, as she began to trade in salt, fish, wine, grain and timber – and, from the sixteenth century, spice, cloth, silk and copper. Longer-distance voyages were launched to Brazil and the Far East.

War, never normally good for economic growth, brought with it a silver lining for the Dutch, in the form of a large influx of skilled migrants from French-controlled territory to the south. Pouring into the free republic, it is estimated that by the 1590s, one in ten people in Holland was an immigrant. These new arrivals brought with them know-how, entrepreneurial flair and capital – helping the fledgling textile trade in particular. Over half of the largest depositors at the Bank of Amsterdam were Walloons.*

This combination of independence, free internal markets, international trade and new capital transformed

* Cipolla, C., *Before the Industrial Revolution: European Society and Economy 1000–1700* (1993), p. 268.

the Netherlands from a backwater into a booming economy.

A SOPHISTICATED ECONOMY

The Dutch prospered by processing tobacco, weaving silk, refining sugar and making everything from bricks to watches, glass to guns, maps to beer. And all for a mass market.

Free from the Habsburgs, the merchant interests that ran Dutch towns ran them in the interests of the productive. Taxes on trade and commerce were cut. The Spanish vice of granting special commercial privileges to the well connected was ended. From the 1590s, guild restrictions were eased and restrictive practices abolished.

No longer running the risk of having it expropriated, as Dutch merchants accumulated capital, they invested it – intensifying the boom. In 1602, Holland became home to the world's first modern stock market: the Amsterdam Stock Exchange.

Capital was invested in new ventures and new technology. While earlier Italian inventors did little more than toy with the idea of water-powered frames for producing yarn, the Dutch pioneered new windmill technology. Wind, alongside a plentiful supply of peat, provided the energy input for this industrial take-off. By the early

1600s, there were thousands of windmills, including industrial ones used to power timber saws, grain presses, paper mills, textile frames and even the production of dyes.

Dutch productivity increased and production rapidly expanded. There were three sugar refineries in Amsterdam in 1603. By 1660, there were sixty. Leiden produced 30,000 pieces of cloth in 1585. By 1665, she was making 140,000 a year. Dutch workers were producing so much more efficiently than anyone else, that they commanded high wages.

Urbanization – in part, enabled by a free labour market – intensified the gains of industrialization and trade. By the seventeenth century, the Netherlands was easily the most urban country in the world, with over half her population living in towns and cities.* Dutch ports became great centres of shipping and commerce. So much so, in fact, that a Venetian diplomat lamented how Amsterdam was 'the image of Venice in the days when Venice was thriving'.†

As Venice had done in an earlier age, the Dutch had discovered the trick of earning a living through specialization and exchange. Despite not producing much in the

---

* Kennedy, P., *The Rise and Fall of the Great Powers* (1987), p. 68.

† Cipolla, C., *Before the Industrial Revolution: European Society and Economy 1000–1700* (1993), p. 267.

way of grain, wine, wool or wood, the Dutch, observed the Italian traveller Lodovico Guicciardini, ate more bread, drank finer wines and dressed in better textiles than those that did.*

Describing what made the Dutch so wealthy, Daniel Defoe explained that they were '... the carryers of the World, the middle Persons in Trade... they buy to sell again, take in to send out; and the greatest part of their vast Commerce consists in being supply'd from all parts of the World, that they may supply all the World again'.†

Dutch living standards duly soared. Per-capita output in 1500 was at about the European average of US$761 (using Angus Maddison's constant prices, again) – which was below the standard of living enjoyed by people in Italy in the last days of the Roman Republic. A century later, in 1600, Dutch output had almost doubled to US$1,381. By 1700, it was almost US$2,130.

Nor were the social benefits of the Dutch Golden Age confined to economic prosperity. Science and learning flourished, too. There were twelve university-type institutions within the Republic, including the University of Leiden. In the seventeenth century, it is estimated that twenty-five out of every thousand young men had a

---

* Cipolla, C., *Before the Industrial Revolution: European Society and Economy 1000–1700* (1993), p. 265.
† Defoe, D., *A Plan of the English Commerce* (1728).

university education. Nowhere in Europe was this percentage higher until the First World War.

A century and a half after the Dutch had begun their upward trajectory, England's output per person began to rise, too. Being a much larger country on the other side of the North Sea, and home to many historians, England's take-off came to overshadow the Dutch in more ways than one. Yet it is a measure of how far ahead the Dutch were, that well into the nineteenth century, almost two hundred and fifty years after output per person in England had started to increase, she still had not caught up with the Dutch.

WHY THE DUTCH?

The Dutch flourished because they were free, the productive able to escape the grip of the parasitic. But why were they free? Why was power dispersed in this one particular part of Europe at this time and not in, say, Portugal or Poland?

The Dutch Golden Age cannot simply be explained away as a question of coincidence, the happy confluence of geography (all those waterways) and power politics (defeating Phillip II). Nor is it enough to merely point to the shape of sixteenth- and seventeenth-century Dutch institutions.

The institution of serfdom might well have disappeared from the Dutch countryside, and municipal authorities were strong. Towns did indeed have autonomy over taxes and commercial affairs, while the *Stadtholder* and States General were kept weak. But all this came about because the old ideas that would have once enabled those with power to use it to extort from the productive had been undermined by new ways of thinking.

As we have seen, when parasitic interests prevail, those at the apex of society are able to order society to their advantage when it is believed that society ought to be ordered. When it is believed that the world and our place in it is part of a celestial order, arranged from on high, we implicitly accept that there should be orders from on high. But in the Netherlands, the notion of a divinely choreographed cosmic order had begun to crumble. This was the great, transformative change that set the Dutch free, for it was what inhibited those that might otherwise inhibit free exchange.

The German priest Martin Luther (1483–1546) had launched a religious revolution – the Reformation – in the early sixteenth century. Luther rejected the idea of a hierarchical Church presiding over a cosmically ordained order. Man's relationship with God, he proclaimed, is direct, 'by faith alone'. The Protestant Reformation saw the creation of all sorts of self-governing religious communities across northern Europe, and nowhere more so than in Holland. These were independent from the hierarchy of popes and bishops.

Today, we might make the mistake of assuming that any questions about church governance are merely an ecclesiastical affair. But in the sixteenth and seventeenth centuries there was nothing other-worldly about such matters. They were of profound political importance. If a religious community could govern itself free from priests, then surely other communities could run their own affairs free from princes? And if a society was capable of organizing itself, why have a powerful king in control at all?

Such disruptive ideas swirled across northern Europe. So subversive of the existing order were they, that in Germany, tens of thousands of peasants rose up during the Peasants' Wars in the early sixteenth century. Unlike the Netherlands, where the Protestant lower orders drove out a Catholic elite, in Germany, the peasant rebellion failed.

If the German sociologist Max Weber is to be believed, the Protestant Reformation is important in explaining intensive economic growth because it brought with it a particular 'work ethic'. But it's difficult to believe that any sort of Protestant work ethic can explain why some parts of Europe started to industrialize.

For a start, there were plenty of passionately Protestant places in Europe in the sixteenth century that showed absolutely no signs of industrialisation. Nor is there much evidence of any proto-Protestantism among say, proto-capitalist northern Italian towns in the fourteenth and fifteenth centuries.

Weber, it seems, has things back-to-front. Protestantism is significant not because it meant the emergence of a peculiarly orderly attitude to work, or anything else. Its significance was the *disorderly* effect it had on established authority. Protestantism is important in explaining why it was that the Dutch came to repudiate the idea of a single set of canonical truths – a 'top-down prescription by which we should live'.* This in turn helps explain why it was that they revolted. But there is much more to Dutch ideas than revolting Protestantism.

Before even Luther came Erasmus of Rotterdam (1466–1536), who did so much to revive rationalism as a way of explaining the world. Then, in the wake of the Dutch revolt, rationalist thinkers began to make Holland their home. The Frenchman René Descartes (1596–1650) lived in the Dutch Republic for twenty of the most productive years of his life. The Englishman John Locke found refuge there from Stuart England. As important as these imports, perhaps, was the homegrown talent, which included Baruch Spinoza (1632–77), for whom God was impersonal – a deterministic system through

---

* Ridley, M., *The Evolution of Everything* (2015), p. 8.

which everything happened by necessity, rather than divine direction.

In place of the old orthodoxies, free inquiry began to bubble away. Hugo Grotius started to build a powerful theological justification for free trade and economic self-order. The merchant class in the Netherlands were no longer supplicants to kings, their autonomy now deemed to be ordained. The natural order was no longer submission, but autonomy. These new ideas encouraged the notion that the merchant class – the *Regenten* – might rule in their own right. The productive had been set righteously free.

13

ENGLAND AND AMERICA

The English, like the Dutch, came to acquire each of the key ingredients needed to produce intensive economic growth: independence from external predators, dispersed power to constrain internal parasites and interconnectedness to allow specialization and exchange.

Unlike the Dutch, England had coal, rather than just wind and peat, to power it all – which is one of the reasons why the English achievement overshadowed the Dutch.

FROM A GLORIOUS REVOLUTION
TO AN INDUSTRIAL ONE

Long independent, the English had a history of imposing constraints on their kings. The Common Law tradition meant that the law was determined by what had gone before, not by the whim of the current monarch. Most famously, in 1215 King John had his wings clipped by the barons who forced him to sign the Magna Carta. Think of it a little bit like the *promissore* contract that the Venetians imposed upon their Doge.

Yet it's important not to overstate the extent to which the power of English kings was limited. For all the charters and supposed constraints, the Tudor strongman, Henry VIII, had freely expropriated and extorted in the 1540s, debasing the currency and seizing what he wanted, just like any other parasite. England remained a relatively poor and backward island off the coast of Europe.

It was not until the extraordinary upheavals of the seventeenth century that monarchical absolutism came into conflict with the insurgent power of Parliament. The victorious Parliamentarians defeated Charles I in battle before beheading him in 1649 – although they did not complete the job of ousting the Stuarts until 1688, when they deposed his son, James II.

William of Orange, the new monarch, was bound by a Bill of Rights passed by Parliament in 1689. In 1701 the Act of Settlement placed further constraints upon the crown, preventing a monarch from waging non-defensive wars without Parliament's permission and limiting the king's ability to appoint whomever he wanted to public office.

It is no coincidence that the Glorious Revolution was followed by the Industrial Revolution. The former was the essential precursor of the latter. England's new Whig elite might have been an oligarchy, but they were a far cry from the absolutist monarchy of the old order. Increasingly, producers were protected from the parasitism of the ruling classes.

At the start of the seventeenth century, there had been over 700 monopolies sold by the crown. Awarded by the king in return for money, they controlled the manufacture and sale of everything from soap and starch to bricks, buttons, coal and iron. In 1623, early on in its struggle against absolutism, Parliament had tried to abolish these restrictions with the Statute of Monopolies. By the end of the seventeenth century, almost all had gone.

A series of seventeenth-century court cases removed many of the medieval restrictions on labour and diminished the power of the guilds. Already, from 1614, an apprentice in one trade was free to work in another.*

Tax extortion became a thing of the past. At the beginning of the seventeenth century, a Stuart monarch had imposed ship money – theoretically a tax to fund the navy – on the merchant class. By the end of the seventeenth century, Parliamentary approval was required before any

* Jones, E., *The European Miracle: Environments, Economies and Geopolitics in the History of Europe and Asia* (1981) p. 99.

taxes could be imposed. Taxes were also removed from production. The hearth tax, which had been an impost upon the productive in some of the nascent cottage textile industries, was abolished in 1689 with the arrival of the new, pro-the-productive regime.

In 1694, the Bank of England was established. This helped ensure that credit was not restricted to the king's cronies, as had happened before. Records from one London bank in the early decades of the eighteenth century show that capital was increasingly allocated to merchants and businessmen that needed it, not simply lords and aristocrats with the political connections to demand it.*

The consequences of all this show up unmistakably in the data on per-capita output. By the mid-seventeenth century, despite the turmoil of war, output per person in England began to rise after centuries of stagnation. Per-capita output has increased in almost every decade since, with the acceleration becoming more marked from the end of the eighteenth century.

As Adam Smith noted a century later: 'In Great Britain industry is perfectly secure; and though it is far from being perfectly free, it is as free or freer than in any other part of Europe.'

---

* Acemoğlu, A., and Robinson, James A., *Why Nations Fail: The Origins of Power, Prosperity and Poverty* (2012), p. 195.

OPEN TO TRADE

Britain also had the third ingredient needed for intensive growth. It was interconnected – both internally and externally. New turnpike roads and canals cut the cost of transport, not only making it easier for producers to bring their goods to market, but also facilitating regional specialization. The ability to access a wide variety of goods through exchange enabled cities to specialize in the industry in which they were most competitive – exploiting comparative advantage, just like the Dutch. Daniel Defoe could see the signs of specialization everywhere in his *Tour Through the Whole Island of Great Britain*: metal goods in Sheffield, woollens in East Anglia, cotton in Manchester, potteries in Cheshire, glass-making in the Midlands.

It wasn't only England's internal trade network that improved, either. England accessed a vast international network, too. Like the Dutch, she traded with the Baltic and Scandinavia, and with France and Spain. Her commerce with the world beyond Europe expanded too, especially with the West Indies, north America, India and the Far East.

Wider international trade enabled even greater specialization at home. By the start of the eighteenth century, raw cotton was being imported and processed in Lancashire and the north. By the 1790s, there were hundreds of cotton mills, with over 500 textile businesses in Manchester alone.

The combination of fewer restrictions on the free exchange of goods, labour and capital, along with a growing web of trade links made the Industrial Revolution possible. Investment flowed into productive new technology. Labour was divided efficiently, based on market demand. The import of raw materials from around the world freed up resources for specialization in manufacture.

By exploiting her comparative advantage in industry, England became the wealthiest society the world had ever known. If Holland had been the richest place on the planet at the end of the seventeenth century, by the end of the eighteenth it was England. By the late nineteenth century, she accounted for almost a quarter of the world's manufacturing output.

Between 1760 and 1830, the UK was responsible for two-thirds of Europe's industrial output growth, and her share of manufacturing production shot up from 1.9 per cent to 9.5 per cent. By 1860, her output share was up to 19.9 per cent; by 1880, 22.9 per cent.* The UK produced over half the world's iron by 1860, and half its coal. Her energy consumption by 1860 was five times

* Kennedy, P., *The Rise and Fall of the Great Powers* (1987), pp. 149–51.

that of the US or Germany, six times that of France and 155 times that of Russia.*

The United Kingdom by 1860 was responsible for a fifth of the world's commerce, and two-fifths of the world's trade in manufactured goods. But if the English had shot up the development ladder, overtaking the Dutch, there were soon a host of others scrambling up behind them – starting with the recently formed United States of America.

INSTITUTIONS AND IDEAS

England, Holland and Venice imposed various kinds of institutional constraint upon their rulers – a powerful Parliament, States General or Great Council, the Bill of Rights or *promissore*. But it was ideas that ultimately explain why the inhibitors were inhibited.

Thomas Hobbes, the author of *Leviathan*, which was published in 1651 amid the turmoil of the English Civil War, is often introduced to history students as a defender of the idea of a strong sovereign. And he was. His book is a stout defence of the established Stuart order. Powerful kings, Hobbes argued, were an essential bulwark needed

* Kennedy, P., *The Rise and Fall of the Great Powers* (1987), pp. 149–51.

to save society from the kind of chaos that had gone before.

But the point about Hobbes is that in making the case that kings should get the credit for establishing an orderly society capable of advancing, he implies something that was, by the standards of the day, revolutionary. Perhaps more so than anything Erasmus or Luther came up with.

Hobbes' central claim is that progress is a question of our political economy – not, by implication, Providence. How we arranged our society mattered, and we had our own agency. So unnerving were the implications of this, Hobbes – like many who have made the case for self-order – was forced to deny that he was an atheist.

Hobbes argued that life in the past had been solitary, poor, nasty, brutish and short. It was parasitism, he implied, that had held humankind back, since in that pre-historic past there had been 'no place for industry' in a world where 'the fruits of these were uncertain'.

It is worth emphasizing that Hobbes was no advocate for a self-organizing society. For him, rather, a strong sovereign was the answer to the problem of the parasitism that had plagued civilization in the past. But like Luther, he unleashed thoughts that had a momentum of their own. He paved the way for others, like John Locke, to go even further, holding unfettered kings to be part of the parasitic problem.

Like Hobbes, John Locke (1632–1704) believed in

natural rights and equality. He specifically refuted those ideas, widespread at the time, that civil society should be founded on divinely sanctioned order. He rejected the divine right of kings and argued that government had to have the consent of the governed – the implication being that if it did not, it could be legitimately ousted.

Society, Locke suggested, was capable of self-direction, rather than being reliant on the direction of a strong sovereign (as Hobbes advocated). 'Society is produced by our wants and government by our wickedness,' he wrote; 'the former promotes our happiness positively by unifying our affections.'

Back from exile in the Netherlands, Locke and his ideas helped shape what came next. From 1689, the Bill of Rights acted as a kind of contract of constraint between the crown and its subjects. The former agreed to abide by a set of rules that protected the interests of the latter. Monopolies, phased out during the seventeenth century, were not reintroduced. In fact, the courts began to rule against guilds, and in favour of a free labour market.

As Locke's ideas moulded England after the Glorious Revolution in the seventeenth century, they helped write the US Constitution after the American Revolution in the eighteenth.

———

AMERICA

In 1776, the American colonies did what the Dutch had done a century and a half before. They ejected the external parasites – not the Habsburgs but the Hanoverian George III – and established a free republic. Then, in 1787, they adopted a constitution that dispersed power.

Those inclined to overlook the influence that ideas have in the affairs of humankind might still maintain that the institutional arrangements that dispersed power in the Netherlands and England arose by accident. There was little that was accidental about the constitution that America's Founding Fathers spent the long, hot summer of 1787 drafting in a court house in Philadelphia. It separated power between federal and state government, and between different branches of government, with deliberate care.

With the right conditions for take-off, America flourished spectacularly. The fledgling republic did not just prosper. Within a century of its birth, it had become the greatest economy on earth, with its citizens consistently enjoying some of the most elevated living standards anywhere.

In 1800, the United States accounted for a measly 0.8 per cent of world manufacturing output, the process of industrialization having hardly begun in north America. By 1860, she still only accounted for about 7 per cent of manufactured output – far less than China did at the time (albeit at a much higher level in per-capita terms). Yet by 1900, America had experienced explosive growth, accounting for almost a quarter of global manufactured output.*

By the early twentieth century, the United States had overtaken the United Kingdom economically. By mid-century, she accounted for approximately 40 per cent of the world's economic output. Like Golden-Age Holland, the United States does not stand out only as an economic powerhouse either. America's contribution to science and learning are without precedent.

For most of the past century, the United States has been the pre-eminent world economic power. So much so, in fact, that in every decade millions – at times, tens of millions – have moved from every corner of the planet to live there and enjoy the fruits of its remarkable intensive economic growth.

America led the industrial revolution based on coal and railways in the late nineteenth century; the automobile revolution in the early twentieth century; the electronic revolution in the mid-twentieth century, and the digital revolution today.

Europe's most successful colony, America flourished

* Kennedy, P., *The Rise and Fall of the Great Powers* (1987), p. 242–249.

like no other because she had that combination of factors essential for take-off *like no other*: independence; openness to trade, ideas and migrants; and internal safeguards against extortive elites.

'But what about America's history of slavery?' you might well wonder. 'The American republic has been run by its own elites, and didn't they prove as prone to extortion as any other?'

It's true that parasitism in America did not come to an abrupt end in 1776, and this held the freshly forged republic back. America only achieved exponential industrial growth after the abolition of slavery in 1861. At the time slavery was outlawed, the US accounted for about 7 per cent of global manufactured output. Within twenty years, that percentage had doubled to 14 per cent. Within forty years of abolition, the US economy was the leading economy on the planet. The eradication of slavery – perhaps the ultimate extractive institution – seems to have coincided with a great leap in output.

14

GERMANY, JAPAN AND RUSSIA

At the start of the nineteenth century, well over half of all industrial output around the world happened in China and India. In China alone, there was more manufacturing than in the whole of Europe, even after several generations of growth in the Netherlands, England and elsewhere. America, independent for just over two decades, still only accounted at that time for under 1 per cent of manufactured production.

By the end of the nineteenth century, this picture of industrial production had changed dramatically. 85 per cent of manufacturing happened in either Europe, America, Russia or Japan. China and India together accounted for about 8 per cent.

Why were some societies able to adapt to industrialization ahead of others?

STEAM-POWERED TAKE-OFF

Steam engines were *the* big breakthrough. Invented a bit before the nineteenth century, it was then that they started to transform the world.

Steam trains opened up the possibilities of transcontinental travel. Steam ships meant transoceanic trade on an unprecedented scale. Steam was not just important because it powered new transport; *the point was that it powered*. Steam engines enabled heat to be converted into machine power, and in doing so allowed the most extraordinary increase in productivity. No longer was the principle source of power the strength of people or beasts of burden, wind or the water wheel. People could power things using charcoal and coal, and then oil and gas.

If you are a technological determinist, you need look no further. The application of this new energy source is the key factor in lifting people out of poverty. It was what enabled the most extraordinary gains in output in agriculture, transport, textile production and manufacturing.

No matter how good all the other technology, productivity per person cannot rise very far if there isn't enough energy. Until the invention of steam engines, and their application, productive processes – in fields or factories – would always be low-energy. Steam enabled us to rise out of the Malthusian trap by freeing us from what you might call an energy trap.

But why was it that some societies proved better at adapting to the new technology than others? During the nineteenth century, industrial know-how spread rapidly from one part of the world to another. Why was it that some societies proved quick to take up the new technology and production techniques, but not others?

Why did Germany, for example, adapt to steam technology, but not Turkey? Why was Japan able to copy innovations from elsewhere, but not China? Why did Russia begin to industrialize towards the end of the nineteenth century and into the early twentieth, but not Africa?

Yet again, it's a case of some societies having those key characteristics essential for success. Those societies that adapted to the brave new world were invariably those that were able to overthrow the old feudal orders that had dominated them internally. In other words, power was dispersed away from an archaic elite, and the productive were set free – or, at least, more free.

Some societies stayed closed, trying to turn their back on outsiders and their new ways. Other societies, often ending centuries of isolation, chose instead to open up to trade, innovation and new ideas.

———

FEUDAL CONSTRAINTS

It would be hard to think of a place less likely to foster progress at the beginning of the nineteenth century than Germany. She was not even a single country, but rather a mosaic of princely fiefdoms, cut off from each other by high tolls, tariffs and poor communications.

Agricultural workers were tied to the land. Society was divided into status groups – or *Stande* – which reserved certain vocations to people born into particular backgrounds. Merchants were awarded trade monopolies but were not allowed to own land. Industrial crafts were the exclusive preserve of trained craftsmen and their apprentices.

While the Dutch had overthrown their aristocratic overlords in the sixteenth century, in Germany, the Peasants' War had left an almost medieval division of society intact, with distinct orders – lords, peasants, clergy, merchants and artisans. Early-nineteenth-century Germany was still ruled by an elite, who extorted what they could from both peasants and merchants. Trade was constrained by an extraordinarily complex array of tolls and taxes on roads and rivers that made it difficult to carry goods. In 1815, there were thirty-eight different tariff systems, as well as thousands of local river tolls, fees and charges.

To make matters worse, much German territory was vulnerable to invasion and big power politics, as her larger neighbours battled it out against Napoleon. Germany was repeatedly invaded in the first fifteen years of the century.

Japan, too, had been ruled by a feudal oligarchy for centuries – the *daimyo* (territorial lords) and *samurai* (aristocratic warriors). The producers – farmers, artisans and merchants – were subject to extortion as a way of life. The Keian edict of 1649, for example, specifically forbade farmers from eating any rice that they grew, ordering them instead to live off millet and vegetables. The surplus that they produced went to the *samurai* and the *daimyo*, while the farmers themselves endured a subsistence existence.

If Japan, unlike Germany, was less at risk of invasion, what she gained in security she paid for in isolation. Japan was not only cut off from the world but had rulers that deliberately discouraged any outside influences. For much of the sixteenth and seventeenth centuries, Japanese citizens were forbidden from travelling overseas on pain of death, and what little trade did occur – the Dutch were virtually alone with a trading station in Japan – was tightly controlled.

Only those that ruled over Japan were allowed to gain from any interaction with the outside world. As so often, protectionism proved to be a matter of protecting the narrow interests of a few, even if it came at great cost to everyone else.

Not surprisingly, living standards in both Germany

and Japan in 1800 were virtually unchanged from several centuries before.

AN END TO THE OLD ORDER
IN GERMANY

For Germany, the big shock was the Napoleonic invasion. In the first decade of the nineteenth century, it caused turmoil and suffering on a barbaric scale. But it also had the effect of sweeping away some of the smaller statelets – and crucially some of the aristocratic elites – *Junkers* – that lived off them.

In 1809, Prussia abolished serfdom, freeing labourers to earn money for a living. Landowners lost out – at least in the western part of Germany, if not in the east where traditional servility continued until well into the twentieth century. Then, in 1834 came the German customs union, or *Zollverein*. Its big effect was to sweep away many of the local tariffs and tolls that had inhibited trade across Germany. Taking away from local feudal overlords their means of extortion proved to be a slow and painful process, and it was only completed with German unification in 1871 when local jurisdictions were simply dissolved.

Unification also saw the dissolution of many of the restrictive guilds, which since the Middle Ages had imposed all kinds of constraints on local urban economies.

Germany's mosaic of local economies started to merge into a unified economy. Attempts to reimpose constraints on competition and trade failed. Within the German customs union, goods and services could be moved freely for the first time.

At the same time, the laying down of railway lines meant much better internal communication within the customs union. Economic growth followed. Coal production grew from a few million tons in the mid-nineteenth century to 277 million tons by 1914, approximately the same level as England.*

Germany might have lagged behind England initially, but she led the way with the so-called Second Industrial Revolution: the development of electrics, optics and chemicals. By 1914, she had caught up with – even slightly overtaken – Britain, with almost 15 per cent of world manufacturing output.

Her scientists and industrialists pioneered new methods of forging steel. Advances in chemistry gave rise to industrial processes that produced dyes, fertilizers and pharmaceuticals. By 1914, over 90 per cent of industrial chemicals were produced in Germany.

------

* Kennedy, P., *The Rise and Fall of the Great Powers* (1987), p. 210.

THE MEIJI REVOLUTION IN JAPAN

Japan's Meiji restoration of 1868 was a misnomer. It was less a restoration than a revolution. Up until that moment, the Tokugawa clan had for centuries run the country as a collection of fiefdoms. Then they went the way of the Stuarts in England and the *Junkers* in Germany.

Just as had happened in England and Germany, sweeping away the old order meant removing the system of monopolies and trade restraints that had been built up. Feudal fiefdoms, *han*, were abolished. No longer the private preserve of the *daimyo*, they became prefectures, administrated in part locally and in part from the centre.

Japanese peasants no longer had to pay 40 per cent of their produce to parasitic *samurai* and overlords, but instead sent taxes to the imperial government. The *samurai* might have attempted a counter-coup in 1878, when they assassinated one of the chief architects of change, Okubo Toshimichi, but their days as an elite living at the expense of merchants and peasants were over.

Even before the overthrow of the old order, Japan had started to open herself up to outside influences after centuries of self-imposed isolation. In 1868, the radical *rangakusha* officials, who supported the new order, opened Japanese ports to foreign trade. In 1871, a delegation was sent to Europe and America to assess how modernity had elevated those societies. They returned full of enthusiasm for reform, and Japan consciously set out to imitate what was seen to have worked in the West.

Consequently, Japan began to industrialize – and specialize. Between 1886 and 1894, thirty-three new mills were founded, mostly in the Osaka area. By the end of the century, Japanese mills were producing 355 million pounds of yarn. By 1913, production had almost doubled – amounting to a quarter of the world's cotton yarn output. Japan was one of the first countries in the world to switch to electrification.

To be clear, even at the outbreak of the First World War, Japan was not an industrial titan. Her output was not much greater than Italy's. But significantly, Japan was the first Asian state to begin to catch up with the West. And that was because she was the first Asian state to have the key ingredients needed for intensive growth.

It was precisely because Japan was able to adapt – overthrowing the Tokugawa order, consciously setting out to emulate others – that she was able to retain her independence. Yet being independent from others is also what kept her free from outsiders.

Compare the fate of Japan in the nineteenth century to virtually every other Asian society. Indonesia had been colonized in the seventeenth century; much of India was gobbled up by England in the eighteenth century; large parts of southeast Asia were claimed by France in the nineteenth; China was divided into different Western powers' spheres of influence. By 1900, aside from Japan, the only countries in Asia not ruled by outsiders were Thailand and Bhutan.

RUSSIA – AN EXCEPTION THAT
PROVES A RULE

Russia did not have a successful revolution in the nineteenth century. Unlike Prussia or Japan, the old established order remained in place. To be sure, there were some concessions to modernity. Serfdom in a legalistic sense was abolished in Russia as it had been in Prussia, even if in practice vast numbers of peasants remained tied to the landed estates on which they worked. There were moves towards 'constitutionalism', or limiting the authority of the Tsar. But what was more notable is how little changed.

Russia had none of the internal changes that Prussia and Japan underwent in the nineteenth century. While she had started to industrialize – laying down lots of railways, for example – she remained relatively backward and overwhelmingly agrarian. Feudal or semi-feudal constraints remained in place, with consequences that proved catastrophic for the old order.

Faced with external pressure during the First World War (agrarian Russia performed disastrously against

Germany and Austria) and internal pressure from dissatisfied industrial workers in her large cities, the Tsarist system eventually came crashing down.

Precisely because Russia had not embarked on the path of overthrowing the old feudal order, opening up to outside influences and exchange, she stagnated. She is the exception that proves the rule. Output per person in Russia on the eve of the First World War was little different to what it had been at the end of the eighteenth century.

If Germany and Japan, however, seemed set securely on the path to progress in the early years of the twentieth century, they – and Russia – were soon to veer off towards a form of totalitarian dictatorship. Instead of progress, they produced death and destruction on an industrial scale.

15

THE FRAGILITY OF PROGRESS

Human progress is neither linear, nor irreversible. History has seen some spectacular regressions.

Back in the fifth century BC, Athens lost the Peloponnesian War to Sparta. A sophisticated, advanced city-state that encouraged trade, innovation and ideas was overwhelmed by a state noted for its military discipline and savagery. The rule of Thirty Tyrants – a pro-Sparta oligarchy – was imposed on a free republic.

Four centuries after the end of the Roman Republic, the western part of the Roman Empire fell. The population and living standards around much of the Mediterranean and across most of Europe plummeted. Advanced technology gave way to the more rudimentary. Towns were abandoned. Levels of literacy reverted to what they had been centuries before.

On other occasions, decline was less dramatic – a case of relative, rather than absolute, decline. During the Middle Ages, advances under the Abbasid in Iraq and the Song in China simply petered out. Venice, which once shone brightly, ceased being quite so exceptional, becoming just another city-statelet. She was certainly nothing exceptional by the time Napoleon ordered her surrender.

There have been Spartas and tyrants, dictators and barbarians in modern times, too.

MODERN BARBARISM

Stefan Zweig was born into a wealthy middle-class family in Vienna in 1881. His father had made money in textiles, and they were typical of the kind of prosperous bourgeois family that the Industrial Revolution had created during the second half of the nineteenth century.

Zweig graduated in 1904 from the University of Vienna, a distinguished seat of Western rational thought, before embarking on a career as a writer. During the 1920s and 1930s, he became one of the most popular writers in the world.

Everything about that world for the first few decades of Zweig's life suggested progress and permanence. It was, he later wrote, a 'golden age of security'. Vienna, his home, had been 'an international metropolis for 2,000 years'. But the world for Zweig, and for millions of others whose lives had been enhanced in almost every conceivable way over the previous few generations, fell apart.

Jewish, Zweig was forced to 'steal away from Vienna like a thief in the night'. His books, once beloved by millions, were burnt. He found exile in England and the New World. But millions of Jews who did not flee were murdered in the years that followed. Millions perished.

In 1942, Zweig killed himself in despair. Europe – where the miracle of modernity had begun – had become a continent of savagery. Zweig's *The World of Yesterday*, the manuscript which he sent to his publisher the day before he took his own life, is a lament for the past – and a timeless reminder to us that there is nothing inevitable about improvements in the human condition.

Zweig's story is proof that productive civilization is more fragile than we sometimes care to understand. And there were millions of individuals like Zweig, whose tragic stories have simply never been told.

Germany – and indeed Japan – might well have modernized in the nineteenth and early twentieth centuries. Their output per person might have soared dramatically, with remarkable increases in productivity. But in the early 1940s, that would hardly have seemed an unequivocal win for human progress.

195

Nazi Germany's wars of conquest, from 1938 onwards, imposed parasitism across (almost) an entire continent. German administrations were forced on occupied territories. Eastern Europe and France were run as a massive estate, producing for the greater good of the Fatherland. As the war progressed, parasitism became mass dehumanization. Millions of workers were enslaved. The most extraordinary atrocities were committed. Millions of Jews, Gypsies and others were murdered on an industrial scale.

As Japan industrialized in the first three decades of the twentieth century, economic power was increasingly concentrated in the hands of the *zaibatsu* – meaning literally 'wealth-clique'. These were family-controlled industrial conglomerates, with monopolies and banking subsidiaries attached. Rather like many of the big businesses in 1930s Germany, the *zaibatsu* entered into agreements with the government. They predominated in mining, chemicals, metals and the merchant fleet, and supplied the army with the weapons to wage war.

Under the Meiji settlement, the Japanese army was only accountable to the emperor, not the civilian government. Indeed, during the 1920s, civilian administrations came to depend on the backing of an increasingly nationalistic officer corps that ran the army. By the 1930s, the army was in effective political control. In October 1941, Hideki Tojo, a Japanese general, took over as prime minister.

Less than two months later, he gave the order to launch the unprovoked assault on Pearl Harbour.

Japan, like Germany, imposed a command economy over the territories that it conquered. The neighbourhood was annexed and millions killed. Like Spartan slaves, the Helots, survivors were set to work for the greater good of the conquerors.

ECONOMIC UNDERPERFORMANCE

When wandering tribes from outside the empire settled inside Roman provinces, the old way of life disappeared. Much of Europe reverted to a subsistence existence. That wasn't what happened when the twentieth century barbarians took over. However horrific, totalitarian regimes managed, for a time at least, to increase economic output compared to what went before. They even managed certain kinds of innovation, albeit ones associated with waging war and killing people. Doesn't this, however, present a problem for us if we define progress simply in terms of output per person?

Of course, there is much more to a civilized society than economic indices. As we noted in an earlier chapter, civilized standards, attitudes and other intangibles are enormously important, too. It's not possible to talk about human progress without taking into account a broad range of what one might call humanitarian considerations.

But we should not let totalitarian regimes off the hook by focusing on all that if it means conceding any economic ground to them. Totalitarian regimes that use command and control policies are not much good at increasing per-capita output in the longer run, either. Like those that ruled over the giant *latifundia* farms in imperial Rome, or the *jagir* estates in Mughal India, they could increase output by the use of force but it is unlikely to be sustainable in the long term.

To be sure, we do not know how the economies of the Third Reich or Tojo's Japan might have performed had either regime managed to somehow survive the 1940s, and existed in peace in the 1950s and beyond. Both disappeared in the rubble of shattered cities.

But we do know what happened to that other totalitarian regime, the Soviet Union – and it's clear that its command and control economy initially produced some substantial increases in output, followed by economic stagnation and failure.

Many of the increases in output in the Soviet system happened as a consequence of a shift from agricultural to industrial production. There may well have been similar windfall gains when the Soviets switched from a war economy, which concentrated on the production of armaments, to one that produced more household goods.

What is clear is that by the 1960s, the Soviet economy had started to slow dramatically and further increases in output per person proved elusive. Collectivized agriculture was never as productive as official statistics seemed to show. Perhaps because economic output within the Soviet system was seen as an end in itself, rather than as a response to meet actual demand, the allocation of resources was inefficient.

One feature of the Soviet system, evident to some outside observers by the 1970s, was that workers within it were consistently less productive and had lower standards of living than those elsewhere. Across much of central Europe, the Soviets had to erect walls to prevent workers voting with their feet and moving to the capitalist West.

To achieve increased output, the Soviet state had to reduce much of the workforce to the status of Soviet Helot. Individuals had little choice as to where they worked, what occupation they had or what terms and conditions they received in return for their efforts. Eventually, the failure of the workers' paradise to deliver for its own workers became so self-evident that it collapsed.

NO END OF HISTORY

At the end of the Cold War, Francis Fukuyama wrote *The End of History*, an anthem to optimism. With the end of the Soviet system, Fukuyama suggested that the world was moving inexorably towards greater liberal democracy. We might each get there at different times, via different routes, but the end destination was the same for the whole of humanity. But is this really the case? Does history unfold as a progression, rather than a set of random events?

Look for too long at Maddison's data about global output per person, and it's possible to get the idea that we are on an unstoppable path of progress. But maybe progress only feels inevitable because we happen to be living through good times? If you lived in Rome in the second century, or Zweig's Vienna in the late nineteenth, you might also have begun to see progress as permanent.

Maybe times are only good when the 'right' side wins the wars? When the Athens rather than the Spartas are ascendant?

England, America, Germany, Japan and Russia all industrialized. Perhaps the world today is only as benign as it is because the Anglo-American side, not Nazi Germany or Tojo's Japan, won the Second World War, and then prevailed against Communist Russia in the Cold War? In 1941, or indeed 1961, there did not seem to be much inevitable about those outcomes.

The world order that exists at Fukuyama's end of history is essentially American-made, underpinned by US military might. Could it be that the world we live in today is a product not of any inevitable historical process, but a (Dutch-)Anglo-American success story spread over the past three or four centuries that has gone global?

The *laissez-faire*, anti-absolutist side won the world's first global war, the Seven Years' War (1756–63). Lincoln's Union prevailed over the Confederacy. Between 1914 and 1918, English, French and eventually American troops wore down the Kaiser's forces. Between 1939 and 1945, the Allies defeated the Axis. But just imagine if the other side had won any of those conflicts. Is it really ideas that enable us to be free, or merely the right kind of might?

PART V

WHAT SET
SOCIETIES FREE

16

THE ENLIGHTENMENT AND UBER-RATIONALISM

I t's an extraordinary story, isn't it? Beginning in the seventeenth century, people living in the Netherlands started to grow rich by taking specialization and exchange to a whole new level. Instead of localized self-sufficiency based around farms and villages, towns started to trade far and wide, creating a regional – and eventually a global – trading system.

Others followed. In the eighteenth century came first the English and then the Americans. In the nineteenth, the Germans and the Japanese started to go through a similar process.

First, the established internal order was overturned – out went the Habsburgs, the Stuarts, the Hanoverians, the *Junkers* and the Tokugawa clan. In came outside influences and exchange. In the wake of each upheaval, the productive were freed from the feudal. Trade, growth and industrialization followed.

Societies in which the productive are set free flourish. But are we any closer to understanding why some societies are free, while others continue to be ruled over by parasitic elites?

THE ENLIGHTENMENT

It's not, as we have seen, simply down to the shape of a society's institutions. Extractive though institutions might be in societies controlled by small elites, it is ideas that ultimately facilitate such extortion. Ideas, not institutions, account for why some societies are free, while others remain feudal.

The rebellious Dutch didn't just overthrow an old extractive elite; they repudiated an older way of thinking, too. Holland ousted the Habsburgs because she was full of self-governing religious communities and towns, and home to radical thinkers and rationalist thought.

It is only possible to properly appreciate the English or the American revolutions if one has some insight into how the insurgents thought. They might have been separated by a century and an open ocean, but both sets of rebels were animated by similar sorts of ideas, often those that emanated from Hobbes and Locke.

There has seldom been a shortage of clever people on hand to explain that it's clever people who account for human progress. Ever since the eighteenth century, a whole string of philosophers – among them, Hume, Kant and Montesquieu – made much the same point about reason underlying our elevation. In our own time, Steve Pinker attributes the progress that has happened in the nineteenth and twentieth centuries to the eighteenth-century Enlightenment that preceded it.

Are they right? Was it the Enlightenment that set societies free and allowed them to flourish?

The age of Enlightenment – *le siècle des Lumières* – saw a series of major scientific advances, extending our understanding of the natural world. From the motion of the stars to basic chemistry, people found rational ways of explaining the world around them. What had once seemed inexplicably mysterious, if not magical, could be understood through science. This undermined traditional structures of authority, belief and scientific thought.

Before the eighteenth century, it had been widely believed that everything worth knowing was known, and was enshrined in authoritative texts: The Bible or the Koran, the Torah or the teachings of Confucius. As the eighteenth century unfolded, some started to appreciate that knowledge is in fact acquired cumulatively. Not all that can be known is yet known. Whether this was a consequence or a cause of scientific discovery can be argued either way. What is definite is that there was a slow corrosion of the old certainty of knowledge, and the previous insistence on authority.

Think of the Enlightenment as a kind of rebellion, or what physicist and philosopher David Deutsch calls a rejection of authority in regard to knowledge. People came to appreciate that not everything that could be known was known. It encouraged people – as in the words of the newly-founded Royal Society's motto, *Nullius in verba* – not to take anyone's word for it.

Reason replaced custom and fairy tale as a source of authority. Instead of deferring to kings, people started to insist on the authority of the people. Centuries of rule in accordance with custom and privilege gave way to rule-making on the basis of what could be deduced to work.

Soon after these subversive ideas began to percolate through certain European societies, there followed a dramatic increase in output per person. *Post hoc ergo propter hoc*. The rationalist revolution in the eighteenth century must, many suppose, have caused the industrial one in the nineteenth and beyond.

———

THE LIMITS OF
THE ENLIGHTENMENT

One of the problems with the theory that the eighteenth-century Enlightenment put us on the path to progress is that the chronology doesn't fit quite as neatly as is sometimes supposed.

If the eighteenth-century Enlightenment made possible the progress that followed, what are we to make of earlier advances? Should we simply overlook the fact that the Dutch, for example, achieved an even earlier industrial revolution? All too often, that is precisely what has happened.

Dutch economic development in the sixteenth and seventeenth centuries – despite being precocious, and the first sustained increase in per-capita output in any large human society since the fall of Rome – is often simply ignored. Perhaps this is partly down to the bias of English-language historians. But it also reflects the fact that there is something rather awkward about a process of take-off that clearly precedes the eighteenth-century Enlightenment.

If forced to account for the so-called 'Dutch Golden Age', many historians end up treating it almost as though it were an accident. A one-off, rather than a harbinger of the progress that was to come. Or else, rather than write up Dutch economic development as being about innovation and ingenuity, they argue that improvements in Dutch incomes were somehow all a consequence of extortion in the East – even though Dutch per-capita output increased before the acquisition of empire.

And what about those even earlier examples of societies that achieved sustained increases in per-capita output? Are they to be downgraded to fit the Enlightenment-explains-everything narrative as well?

Venice, which was for several centuries in a league of her own economically and technologically, is often treated by historians as just another northern Italian city-state, exceptional only by being built on water. As with the Dutch, the extent of her achievement is an awkward fact for those that insist it wasn't until the eighteenth-century Enlightenment that progress became possible.

Some try to get around such inconvenient chronology by extending the 'century of lights' back into the seventeenth century and earlier, incorporating Renaissance and medieval humanists, too. How many early Christian thinkers do we need to accept helped lay the foundations of Western thought before we give up on the idea that the eighteenth century alone gave rise to rationalism, or that rationalism alone accounts for human progress?

It's not even as if the eighteenth century was the first time that new ideas had begun to erode Europe's established order of princes and priests. Two hundred years before the collapse of the *Ancien Régime* in France, the Protestant Reformation had triggered a bloody series of uprisings against hereditary hierarchy in Germany. The leaders of the Peasants' armies in early-sixteenth-century Germany issued their Twelve Articles demanding the abolition of princely and priestly privilege long before Rousseau wrote about the Rights of Man.

Extending the Enlightenment back into the Middle Ages stretches credibility. Incorporating antiquity into it would be ridiculous. So, what is one to make of the clear, compelling evidence of a sustained increase in per-capita output in the Roman Republic – unsurpassed for over a millennium? Should we see Rome's ascendency as merely a matter of conquest and military endeavour? The Roman Republic enjoyed a rise in living standards due to specialization and exchange, and it's not possible to account for it as simply the accumulation of wealth from overseas provinces. As with the Dutch and the English – although, curiously, not the Americans – empire (whether it proved to be a net contributor to or drain on economic strength) largely came later.

It is only possible to sustain the argument that human progress happened as a consequence of the eighteenth-century Enlightenment if you are prepared to ignore an awful lot of history.

———

A TALE OF TWO REVOLUTIONS

If the Enlightenment set societies free and produced progress, how come things didn't quite work out that way in France, the country at the epicentre of the eighteenth-century rationalist revolution?

Contrast the two dramatic upheavals that happened towards the end of the eighteenth century – the first in America (1765–83) and the second in France (1789–99). Each of these revolts seemed to many at the time to be an expression of a similar phenomenon: a rationalist rising against the old order, with the authority of kings giving way to that of the people. No one seemed more certain of the similarity between the two uprisings than Thomas Paine.

Born in England in 1737, Paine emigrated to America just in time to take part in the insurrection there. His pamphlet, *Common Sense*, brilliantly articulated the case of the rebel colonies against the crown. He was widely read and, after the war, went on to become one of the Founding Fathers of the new republic. Shortly afterwards, on the other side of the Atlantic in France, Louis XVI's rule of rent-seeking luxury came crashing down. Years of exorbitant taxes imposed on the peasantry had taken their toll. Just as ideas about universal rights had started to percolate through French society, undermining deference and hierarchy, the masses rose in revolt.

The effect was explosive. In July 1789, a Parisian mob stormed the Bastille and the *Ancien Régime* fell. Feudalism was abolished, and new rights and a republic proclaimed. So enthusiastic was Paine in his support of what was happening in France that he hurried over to be part of it, too, becoming a French citizen and an elected member of the new Assembly. Yet Paine's fate demonstrates rather magnificently quite how different these two insurgencies – and the ideas behind them – really were.

After the old regime was ousted in America, Paine had sat down alongside the other Founding Fathers to draft a new constitution. They had plenty of passionate arguments crammed into that Philadelphia court house during the summer of 1787. But the ringleaders of America's republican revolt did not attempt to cart each other off to the guillotine as they did in France.

In Paris in the aftermath of the revolution, one Jacobin faction tried to systematically slaughter the other, *Montagnards* pitched against *Girondins*. Paine in post-revolutionary Paris was arrested and sentenced to death. He only narrowly escaped with his life when Robespierre, leader of the faction trying to have him guillotined, fell from power. Imagine, for a moment, if on the other side of the Atlantic, Benjamin Franklin had tried to have John Adams executed? Imagine if, after a bloodbath, George Washington emerged, Napoleon-like, to declare himself Emperor of America? Or if he had then gone on to establish a hereditary dynasty, invading Canada, Brazil and Mexico and establishing puppet monarchies? That is what happened after the French Revolution. The Napoleonic Wars that followed were amongst the bloodiest episodes in human history.*

The two revolutions in which Paine participated, he came to realize, were animated by profoundly different ideas that took those societies in very different directions.

In post-revolution America, Locke's notion of natural rights meant rights (for white male Americans) held independently of any authority. In post-revolution France, authority claimed legitimacy on the basis that it might impose such natural rights on everyone else.

In America, power was dispersed and constrained. In the aftermath of upheaval, the Founding Fathers obsessed about how to prevent any single person or faction gaining too much power over others. In France, power was concentrated and a dictatorship established. Her post-revolutionary leaders obsessed as to how they might wield power over others in order that they might mould society according to their own conception of reason.

With its cry of '*liberté, egalité, fraternité*', Rousseau's revolt is often – even today – seen as central to the path of

* Pinker, S., *The Better Angels of Our Nature: A History of Violence and Humanity* (2012), p. 195.

progress. But it wasn't. It unleashed a tyrannical blood-bath. Rousseau argued that the interests of the individual and the whole of society could only be reconciled by what he termed a General Will. This led directly to the Terror. In parts of France, such as the Vendée, atrocities were committed on an epic scale.* Frenchmen were forced to prostrate themselves before those who governed in the name of the General Will. Citizens who refused to obey the dictates of reason, wrote Rousseau, must be 'forced to be free'.

Jacobinism is not part of the story of human progress. It was a blood-soaked regression – and proof that rationalism does not necessarily free societies from the grip of parasitic elites. It demonstrated – tragically, not for the last time – that rationalism does not necessarily mean constraints on the powerful, but instead provides a pretext for small elites to exercise power over others.

Man, wrote Rousseau not long before the French Revolution, was everywhere in chains. The Enlightenment might have come along and cast off the old chains of faith, feudalism and hierarchy, but they went on to shackle humankind to something even more terrible.

* See, for example, Reynald Secher, *A French Genocide: the Vendée* (translated by George Holoch), University of Notre Dame Press 2003.

215

An absolutist belief in reason led to the guillotine. It later led to the gulag and the gas chamber.

The overzealous application of rationalism has, since the eighteenth century, produced some of the great reversals of progress in human history. Shortly after Germany, Japan and Russia had started to industrialize, they veered off in a dramatically different direction to that taken by Holland, England and America. They did so because they, like France before them, came under the influence of those who believed in ordering society from above, according to a particular blueprint.

UBER-RATIONALISM

If you believe that rationalism is what produces human progress, you are only a short step away from a dangerous fallacy: the notion that society has to have a rationalist blueprint in order to advance.

Ever since the eighteenth century, that is precisely what has happened. Reason has given rise to the illusion of absolute truth. This has produced certainty where there ought to be scepticism and doubt. Far from just undermining the authority of the old order, uber-rationalism has helped impose a new one. Instead of enabling a spontaneous economic and social order to emerge, it has encouraged small elites to arrange one by design.

It wasn't just the Jacobins. Karl Marx (1818–83) was as much a product of the Enlightenment as any other philosopher. He built on Rousseau's critique of the division of labour, arguing not merely that the division of labour was a cause of unhappiness but that it led to exploitation and class struggle – which was, he suggested, the thing that had really inhibited progress. The leader of the Russian Revolution, Lenin, referred to his communist cadres as 'Jacobins connected to the proletariat'.

Again, a small cadre of true-believers arose, claiming to be in possession of a superior set of truths to which the masses must submit. This priesthood – in the Soviet Politburo rather than the Directory in France – insisted on an authority of knowledge, free from any criticism. Unless this elite was given untrammelled power to act, humankind, they insisted, could not be saved.

Any individual seeking to live on their own terms in such a society was guilty of a kind of secular sin – and often punished accordingly. To act in your own interest was to be condemned as a speculator, or a hoarder, a *bourgeoisie* or a *kulak*. The productive and the merchant class were vilified once again. Lenin, like Robespierre, was hostile to traders and merchants the way most premodern rulers had been.

In most pre-modern societies, the proceeds of what people produced was transferred to an extractive elite. As Bastiat observed shortly after the French Revolution, this was often done by creating a moral code that glorified extortion. In many societies arranged according to the dictates of reason, however, the extractive elites went one better than glorifying forms of taxation. They simply abolished private property altogether, removing at a stroke any claim that an individual might have over what they could accumulate in their own name. What was theirs was the state's, and for state officials to do with as they wished.

In the name of reason, Rousseau insisted that private property was at the root of humanity's failing, with inequality its result. The division of labour, he went on, far from being the engine by which we are elevated, was rather part of a process of degeneration. Marx took this idea even further, explaining history as a conflict between classes.

Societies arranged according to these sort of Enlightenment ideas were, unsurprisingly, not great centres of specialization and exchange. Whatever increases in output achieved by official fiat – and in Russia in particular, orchestrated industrialization – were nothing like the surges in output attained elsewhere.

For at least a millennium before the revolution, France had easily the biggest economy in Europe. She was overtaken by England, Germany and others in the early nineteenth century and has been a second-tier economic power ever since.

Soviet Russia, with a vast population and industrial output, was for a while a great power. But that outward strength, like that of the Ottomans or the Ming, was never matched by internal innovation or by impressive per-capita indices, other than those that measured social decay and despair.

In Germany, grotesque ideas about ordering entire continents by design were promoted by those influenced by thinkers such as Theodor Fritsch and Paul de Lagarde. This led directly to the death of millions. Stefan Zweig was just one of many victims since the eighteenth century when the idea took hold that society is best ordered according to some sort of rationalist design.

Far from explaining why power was dispersed within certain societies, the Enlightenment generated ideas that were just as likely to concentrate it, with murderous consequences.

17

AN INSIGHT THAT CHANGED EVERYTHING

Free societies arise when people stop trying to order human affairs from on high. This happens when it is appreciated that there is no need to do so because it is understood that order is best allowed to emerge spontaneously instead.

For most of human history this was simply not the way most people thought. Instead, in most societies people made sense of the world by imagining there to be intentionality all around them. Our ancestors saw all kinds of extraneous agency, with spirits and supernatural forces behind natural phenomena, from thunder storms to crop failures.

In Mexico, the sun was believed to rise because of the god Huitzilopochtli. In Egypt it was due to Ra. Crops grew in Mesopotamia thanks to Ninurta, and in China if Shennong was satisfied. If the rains came to India, it was because Indra was pleased. Plague and famine in Iraq meant that Erra was angry.

This idea that some supernatural force was calling the shots was remarkably persistent and widespread, and the notion of deliberate design ran through much of Western thought as well. Plato suggested that society worked by imitating a designed cosmic order. Aristotle saw intentionality in inanimate matter. From Homer to Luther, thinkers have thought divine direction was somehow central in the affairs of humankind. Homer records how the gods decided the outcome of battles. Even Luther insisted that our fate was in His hands. Inshallah, you might almost say.

What has been unique about Western thought is that alongside the idea of a divinely orchestrated universe ran a countervailing belief that repudiated the notion of any kind of divine design. Order, this alternative insight suggested, is something that emerges by itself. The world and what is in it happens without any kind of top-down direction.

THE IDEA OF SELF-ORDER IN ANTIQUITY

Sitting alongside Plato and Aristotle, with their ideas of

designed cosmic order and intentionality in inanimate matter, was a strand of Greek thought that rejected any notion of divine design: that of the Epicureans, named after the Greek thinker Epicurus (341–270 BC).

The Epicureans understood that the world and all that was in it was not the product of some grand godly plan but was self-arranging. Gods, in so far as they existed, the Epicureans argued, were distant and uninvolved in the affairs of humankind.*

This Epicurean insight was not marginal to Greek thought – it was central to it. Look at how in *The Iliad* and *The Odyssey*, those two early Greek tales, events were attributed to the actions of gods. By the time Herodotus wrote his *Histories*, events are explained in terms of human agency and action.

The Epicureans drew on even older Greek ideas and insights. Xenophanes (570–475 BC) had rejected mythological accounts of why things were the way they were. Anaxagoras (510–428 BC) argued that reality was composed of physical ingredients blended together in different ways to produce different substances. In about 400 BC, long before any eighteenth-century scientist, Democritus (460–370 BC) suggested that the tiniest matter was made

---

* Interestingly, when Erasmus sought to distance himself from the Protestant agitators, he accused them of being little more than Epicureans.

of atoms – and that everything in existence consisted of various combinations of either atoms or a void. 'Nothing exists except atoms and empty space,' he insisted, anticipating modern physics.

Epicurus drew such ideas into an overarching philosophy, one which saw the world as having emerged spontaneously, a consequence of atoms unceasingly grouping and regrouping. The world was made not by any divine being but by the collision and combination of atoms.

Of course, if everything in the world was created by atoms, with order emerging in this way, where did that leave the idea of God as the grand architect?

Everything, suggested Lucretius, was spontaneous and self-organizing. Long before Charles Darwin, Lucretius advanced the idea that the natural world consisted of different species of animal that had risen through a kind of competition, in which 'those with useful characteristics' survived and those that lacked them were 'brought by nature to destruction'. People too, according to this understanding of the world, were not made by a creator but consisted of complex combinations of atoms. Two thousand years before Hobbes wrote *Leviathan*, Lucretius alluded to human civilization arising out of a primitive, prehistoric past, evolving not through divine direction but our own agency.

Where did all this leave Providence?

Lucretius argued that there was no need to live in

moral fear of divine beings and their vengeance. There was, he suggested, literally nothing to fear – nor indeed to worship. The Epicureans argued instead that the purpose of life was the pursuit of pleasure – by which they meant not sensual hedonism, but self-interest. If there is a higher purpose we are ordained to serve, it is ourselves.

At times, Lucretius' six-part poem, *On the Nature of Things*, articulates ideas that are so thoroughly modern, it is hard to believe that anyone thought that way two thousand years ago. Yet lots of people did. *On the Nature of Things* is but one tiny surviving fragment of a lost Epicurean intellectual tradition that was once widespread around the Mediterranean in antiquity.

What we might loosely call Epicurean insights emanated from Greece. Yet they were also widespread and popular in the Roman world, at least until the third century AD. 'Just when the gods had ceased to be', wrote Gustave Flaubert of this period of Roman history, 'and the Christ had not yet come, there was a unique moment in history… when man stood alone.' Flaubert might have got the timeline a little askew but, for a few fleeting generations, Roman man and woman were indeed free from a sense that extraneous agency was responsible for the day-to-day design, maintenance and moral regulation of the world.

It is in that brief interlude that Roman achievement

stands: institutions existed that constrained the powerful; there were remarkable innovations in engineering and technology; Roman per-capita output by the first century AD rose higher than in any large, settled society until sixteenth-century Holland. It had still not been exceeded in Asia by 1950 or most of Sub-Saharan Africa by 1990. Rome, with over a million inhabitants in the first century AD, was the largest city on earth until China's Hangzhou in the Middle Ages. Roman art and architecture, engineering and technology represented an unmatched pinnacle of human attainment until the early-modern era.

AN INSIGHT ERASED

It is striking how, unlike the work of Plato or Aristotle, not a single piece of Epicurus' writing survives, and almost nothing of Democritus' prodigious output. Indeed, the only reason we know much about the Epicurean school of philosophy at all is down to the survival of a single copy of Lucretius' only work, which turned up – almost miraculously – in the library of a fifteenth-century German monastery.

To be sure, the decay of parchment and papyrus means that the work of most writers and thinkers in the Classical world have disappeared. What we know about some of the greatest minds of the past has only been passed down to us third-hand. It is estimated that three-quarters of Aristotle's work has been lost. The Greek playwright Aeschylus, once extraordinarily well-known, wrote around ninety plays but today only a mere six remain.

Many Greek and Roman works failed to survive down the centuries, and it is notable that the school of thought in antiquity that rejected the idea of divine design was almost entirely extinguished. Plato and Aristotle could, with their notion of intentionality, be accommodated into the teachings of the early Christian church. The ideas of Epicurus could not. A philosophy that taught that order was an emergent phenomenon seemed to have been regarded as an affront.

What was it about Epicurean ideas that was so offensive? Part of it comes down to practical politics. As Rome became an imperial power, a small elite needed to direct ever greater resources and manpower to run what was in effect a war machine fuelled by plunder. This elite needed a creed that enabled them to marshal resources and order the empire from on high.

Initially, emperors attempted to do this by simply declaring themselves divine. From that point on, rulers perhaps had little sympathy for a Greek intellectual tradition that insisted that law and justice needed legitimizing. Or perhaps it was precisely in order to provide them with an ethical underpinning to legitimize the way they ruled that they turned to a new creed. From the time of Constantine,

Christianity became the state-backed religion. Useful for trying to mould together a multicultural, polyglot empire, the new religion conveniently emphasized ideas of divine design and purpose.

Epicurean ideas posed a threat to all this, with their insistence that the world worked fine without any top-down direction. It was perhaps more than a little inconvenient. Old Epicurean ideas and outlooks were attacked and extinguished. Augustine, Ambrose, Lactantius, Jerome and a host of others attacked Epicurean ideas in various tracts and sermons.

With great dishonesty but devastating effectiveness, these sometimes-less-than-saintly propagandists portrayed a belief system that emphasized frugality and simple living as being all about the pursuit of sensual pleasure. It's a misrepresentation that persists to this day (and, incidentally, it explains why in his letter to William Short, Thomas Jefferson still felt the need to refer to the 'genuine' doctrines of Epicurus, as opposed to the 'imputed').

Thus was a philosophy that acknowledged humans as possessing their own agency grotesquely misrepresented as a cult of decadence by those who would rather we submit to their notion of an extraneous agency. For the next thirteen centuries, what had been Roman Europe was preyed upon by parasites who organized society for their own intent and purpose. A Dark Age lasted for centuries, with society reverting back to a subsistence level as parasitic warlords extracted what they could from the productive.

The parasites have waged a long war against the idea of order as an emergent phenomenon. They not only largely extinguished Lucretius' ideas in the first and second century, but they burnt the Italian monk, Giordano Bruno, in the sixteenth century, and Spinoza's books in the seventeenth century. They were still fuming over Darwin in the nineteenth.

AN INSIGHT REINVENTED

It was once believed that farming had originated from a single source, somewhere in the Middle East a few thousand years ago. Today, we know that farming did, in fact, arise entirely independently at different times and in different places. Different people, it seems, can come to the same kind of conclusions. So, too, it seems when it comes to ideas about self-order.

We know that insights about self-order, an essential ingredient for a free society, existed in antiquity. And we know too that such insights were almost entirely extinguished. But how and why did they come back?

Venice in the Middle Ages was not a great seat of classical learning. One simply would not have found any sort of ancient Epicurean texts there before the Renaissance. The Venetians, sadly, would have been more likely to burn any ancient Greek texts that they came across lingering in the libraries of Constantinople, rather than absorb and understand them.

Venice, however, rather like those early south American agriculturalists who learnt how to farm for themselves, discovered something about self-order by accident, if not imitation. How did this happen? Long before anyone had heard of Luther, Venice just happened to have her own autonomous church. From the early days of the republic, the city-state took great care to cultivate the myth that St Mark had established his own church on the Rialto. Venice's ability to arrange her own religious affairs proved to be a critical innovation, yet one that historians often merely note in passing, as if it were simply some kind of local quirk or curiosity, no more remarkable than some of Venice's distinctive architecture.

Having a major-league saint like St Mark found his own church enabled Venice to organize religious matters for herself, by claiming that she and her church had parity with the pope and St Peter in Rome. Being beyond papal jurisdiction in this way helped safeguard Venice's independence. She could and did simply ignore the edicts of popes and emperors. She was able to maintain her own independent foreign and trade policy, within Christendom and beyond. Being able to organize her own religious affairs had all sorts of important implications in terms of creating conditions conducive to economic take-off.

It gave the city-state autonomy in legal matters. Not accepting the overriding authority of a papal or imperial authority elsewhere helped ensure that power within the city-state remained diffuse. It meant it was far harder for the kind of imperial or papal interest to emerge within the city-state, as happened within many other northern Italian cities at the time. As happened in Holland later on, the productive merchant interest was able to prevail.

THE ANCIENT AND MODERN MEET

The Renaissance was indeed a rebirth. It was a time when insights from the classical past that had been long dead, came alive again.

One of the many rediscoveries was, as we have seen, a single copy of Lucretius' *On the Nature of Things*. According to Stephen Greenblatt, the publication of this lost work caused a slow-moving sensation. It was in time to influence Newton, Galileo and many others.*

From it, ideas about atomism started to circulate, and with them the heretical notion of a self-ordering

---

* See Stephen Greenblatt's brilliant, thought-provoking book, *The Swerve: How the World Became Modern* (2011).

universe. As Bruno's unfortunate fate showed, it remained extremely dangerous to articulate these ideas, and yet the implications of them could not be kept in check by any number of inquisitions. The printing press saw to that.

Other ideas about how a self-ordered society might operate began to percolate, too. Polybius' *Histories*, less heretical perhaps with its detailed description of the Roman Republican constitution, was also rediscovered and widely read. In Holland, Spinoza's claim that the world unfolded according to eternal laws, not extraneous whim, had a great deal in common with certain schools of philosophy in ancient Greece, the Stoics as well as the Epicureans. However offensive this idea was to Spinoza's co-religionists (he was exiled from his local Jewish community), he was not advocating atheism any more than Hobbes had. But like Hobbes, the implications of his ideas were far-reaching.

The impact of all these rediscovered insights was not immediate, but their effects can be clearly seen when one compares the outcome of the English revolution in the late seventeenth century with that of the American one a hundred years later.

When Locke returned to England from exile in 1688, intent on overthrowing the old Stuart order, he came not only with a Dutch king but with Dutch ideas too. Locke's revolution boiled down to installing a better king – one with a Dutch appreciation of monarchical minimalism

– rather than finding some sort of alternative. The most important constitutional innovation Locke and his contemporaries came up with was the idea of a Bill of Rights, which if anything seemed a little Venetian. Just like the kind of *promissore* imposed on an incoming Doge, the Bill of Rights was a kind of contract intended to rein in the excesses of a future king.

Contrast that with what happened a century or so later, after the American revolution. The American Founding Fathers were influenced heavily by Locke. So much so, in fact, that they borrowed the idea of a Bill of Rights, incorporating not only the idea but often the actual text, and making it part of their new Constitution in the form of the first ten amendments.

Yet the Founding Fathers also introduced a whole series of innovations that owed nothing to Locke, England or the Netherlands. They weren't in the business of seeking to install an American king to rule over the newly independent colonies. What the Founding Fathers did was try to revive an even grander republican tradition. After almost two thousand years, they sought to resurrect elements of the Roman constitution in the New World. It's why they built a Senate and a Capitol on the banks of the Potomac.

The Founding Fathers had read Polybius and were familiar with the Roman Republican tradition in a way that the Dutch and the English at the time of their upheavals were not. Thus, while the Venetians and the Dutch stumbled across the idea of self-order by accident, and the English attempted it by emulation – importing a Dutch king to rule over them – the Americans achieved it by copying what they knew from the pages of Polybius.

Polybius gave the Founding Fathers the idea of con-straining the powerful by having a series of competing officials, a system of checks and balances, or even a separation of powers, one might say. No single faction or party, Madison and his colleagues hoped, could ever dominate. They put in place safeguards not only against another George III, but against the emergence of an American Caesar or a rabble-rousing *signore*.

Ancient insights about self-order, for so long so periph-eral, had started to take centre stage once again in human affairs.

Thomas Jefferson, one of the Founding Fathers, even called himself an Epicurean. On reading Lucretius, it was, he declared, a summary of 'everything rational in moral philosophy which Greece and Rome have left us'. The American Declaration of Independence, which Jefferson wrote, is not just a rallying cry to the cause of a free peo-ple seeking to govern their own affairs. In its insistence on the inalienable right to 'life, liberty and *the pursuit of happiness*' is there not also an echo of Epicurus?

In the two centuries or so since Jefferson wrote those words, ideas about self-order have gone global.

18

PROGRESS GOES GLOBAL

Most of humankind now enjoys, to some extent or other, the conditions that allow for economic growth: independence from predatory outsiders, openness to trade and exchange, and dispersed power. Two hundred years ago, those conditions existed in a few pockets in north-western Europe and America. Today they are found (almost) everywhere.

INDEPENDENCE (ALMOST) EVERYWHERE

Much of the world used to be divided into different empires. A century ago, India was ruled by the British, Indo-China by France. Almost all of Africa was claimed by one European power or another. Even those parts of the planet not formally controlled by an outside power were often part of an informal empire. China before the First World War, for example, was divided into different spheres of influence: France in the south, Britain in Shanghai and along the Yangtze, Germany around Qingdao and Russia in the north. Much of Europe itself had been incorporated in to one empire or another, too.

But then the European empires fell apart, in both Europe and beyond. Barely able to feed their own population at the end of the Second World War, the Dutch gave up any idea of trying to reclaim their overseas possessions after Japanese occupation ended. Indonesia declared independence in 1945.

India had already agitated for self-rule so that at the start of the Second World War, Britain hung on there by only a thread. Britain formally declared the end of her empire in India in 1947 and rolled things up in Africa in the decade or so that followed. She was out of Malaysia by 1957.

Some European powers, like France and Portugal, tried to cling on, but were defeated in a series of humiliating colonial wars that followed. America – apart from a brief fling with the Philippines that ended in 1946 – had avoided acquiring any empire but got herself entangled in Indo-China after the French left. But even then, the last US army personnel had left by 1976. Russia – whose

Soviet empire was perhaps the last of the great European empires – lost formal control over much of eastern Europe and central Asia in the early 1990s.

Pretty much every part of the planet has in one way or another undergone something a little like the Dutch had from 1581 or the Americans in 1776. That is to say, the outsiders who ruled over them have been ousted. There are, of course, some important exceptions – it's possible to find places around the planet, like Western Sahara or Catalonia, where some local people still believe that they are occupied by, or at least have been unjustly incorporated into, a foreign power.

But for all these exceptions, most societies have at least the first essential ingredient for success: independence. But independence alone has never been enough to produce progress and prosperity. If a society simply swaps external predators for internal parasites it can even find itself worse off.

INDEPENDENCE IS NOT ENOUGH

China had, for the better part of a century, been treated abominably by outside aggressors. Weakened by her rulers from within, a series of outside powers were able to impose on her a series of one-sided treaties. Ports were occupied and garrisons maintained, with foreigners claiming the right to levy their own customs. Enclaves and concessions were carved out. Different powers jostled to control the crumbling court of China's last emperors. Then during the 1930s and 1940s, Japan launched a full-scale invasion, annexing territory and causing a calamitous loss of life.

China's expulsion of these outside powers, and their proxies, in the 1940s should be seen as a heroic achievement. Up there alongside Washington at Valley Forge, the Chinese Communists' Long March was a triumph against tyranny. But unlike the Americans after Yorktown, China's new rulers did not then arrange for the dispersal of power within their domains.

After driving out the last of Chiang Kai-shek's troops from the port city of Chengdu and forcing them to flee to Taiwan, China's new rulers imposed a system of centralized control. China's Communists attempted to order every aspect of society from the centre. Land ownership was collectivized; private property abolished. Society was dragooned as surely as it had been under any emperor. Attempts were made to force industrialization through collective efforts at village level. These efforts were disastrous. Forcing people off the land to work in factories meant not enough food was produced. The so-called Great Leap Forward ended in mass starvation.

Perhaps not entirely surprisingly given her recent history, China after the Communist takeover shut herself off from the outside world. Trade was severely restricted. Hong Kong was for many years the only effective *entrepôt* between China and the world beyond. China might have achieved her independence, but in the 1950s and 1960s she seemed very far from achieving any of the other conditions needed to achieve economic take-off. Hundreds of millions of Chinese people lived a subsistence existence. In the early 1960s, famine meant many Chinese lived below even that.

At almost the same time that China drove out the last of the occupying powers, India, too, achieved independence after centuries of foreign rule. India also demonstrated, albeit in a very different way, that independence alone is not enough to ensure economic success. Unlike Communist China, India attained independence as a democracy – and has remained a successful one ever since. Her rulers might, unlike those in Beijing, have had to answer directly to the people – power across post-independence India was never as concentrated as it was in Communist China – but she, too, turned inwards, inhibiting free exchange.

Under Jawaharlal Nehru, a series of disastrous attempts were made to make India's economy self-contained. Massive import taxes were imposed; farming cooperatives were created; government officials made investment decisions. India might have been independent, but closed off from the world economy, her share of world trade fell in the 1950s and 1960s. There were food shortages, and even

239

famines. Worse, Nehru's successor (and daughter), Indira Gandhi, nationalized the banks, and then the coal, iron, steel and even textile industries. Strict regulatory controls were imposed on the private sector so that production of almost anything required permissions and permits.

Almost exactly the same pattern of independence, followed by introversion, happened in Indonesia. Independence was not followed by dramatic progress but by several decades during which a small, self-serving elite inhibited trade and exchange. Under first Sukarno and then Suharto, Indonesia imposed on herself all manner of economic controls. These gave a small number of the politically connected new levers they could pull to extort. Suharto and his entourage did so on an epic scale, siphoning off a fortune. While the president's personal income soared, his fellow countrymen remained poor. It was as if after independence, George Washington or Alexander Hamilton had embezzled Congressional funds, while nationalising the American economy.

By the late 1960s, Indonesia could only feed herself by distributing American food aid. Much of the growth that there was in the 1980s was dependent on oil exports. Between the mid-1960s and mid-1980s, per-capita income growth was slow.

Across much of Sub-Saharan Africa, independence saw an even more rapacious elite take over from foreign powers. Suharto-like strong men emerged in dozens of African states; nations' treasuries were turned into private bank accounts for autocrats; import taxes were erected that discouraged trade. In many nations, among them Ghana and Zaire, per-capita incomes fell in the decades after independence. Some, such as Uganda and Ethiopia, saw decades of turmoil, war and famine. By the mid-1980s, many of Africa's independent states looked like they were failing states.

Not only is it true that independence is not enough. Paradoxically, in Asia, it was those states that weren't fully independent that tended to achieve prosperity first.

OPENNESS

Alone among the Asian states in the nineteenth century, Japan had started to take off economically. She was eventually joined in the mid-twentieth century by a second group of states – South Korea, Hong Kong, Singapore and Taiwan – which from the 1960s began to achieve rapid increases in per-capita output and income.

Why did these four states start to prosper when they did, and why did they start to flourish while many larger Asian states stumbled?

Part of the reason is that they started out under the protective umbrella of a distant power, in much the same way that Venice got going under the suzerainty of remote Byzantium. Each of these four Asian states were either formally – if lightly – ruled by Britain (Singapore until 1965, Hong Kong until 1997) or firmly within an American sphere of influence (Taiwan from 1949 and South Korea from 1950).

As satellites of the Anglo-American powers, these small states were in one sense not fully independent. But as with Venice several centuries earlier, being in the orbit of one big remote power helped ensure that they remained outside the gravitational pull of some of the near neighbours – which might have been looking to absorb them.

Britain ensured that neither Singapore nor Hong Kong were overrun by their more powerful neighbours the way Portuguese Goa was when she was annexed by India in 1961. American firepower kept the Chinese army north of the 38th parallel on the Korean peninsula, and prevented Beijing making any attempt to cross the straits of Taiwan.

Being notionally part of Byzantium meant that Venice was in her earliest days part of a wider, Greek-speaking Mediterranean world. In a similar way, perhaps, through the alliances that they had with their English-speaking patrons, Hong Kong, Singapore, South Korea and Taiwan were able to access investment, capital and technology.

The combined effect of all this was dramatic. Hong Kong, a dilapidated port in the late 1940s, experienced double-digit growth from the early 1950s. Trade and people poured in. Soon, she was a major economic hub. In the early 1950s, Hong Kong's average income was about half of that in the UK. Today it is roughly twice the UK average.

Something similar happened in Singapore. In the mid-1950s, Singapore's per-capita GDP was about half of that in the UK. Today it is roughly twice that of the UK. Taiwan and South Korea experienced rapid growth, too. Often thought of as middle-income countries, both are drawing level with the West in terms of living standards. South Korea is not even a middle-income country any more, but a wealthy industrial nation on a par with Europe and America.

By the 1970s, some of the smaller Asian states had clearly started to pull ahead. From the 1980s, China followed. Then in the 1990s, India, and in the first decade of the twenty-first century, Indonesia and others. They, too, started to open up their economies and put various kinds of constraint on those that ruled them.

DISPERSED POWER

In the late 1970s, a group of Chinese officials in Anhui province realised that they were facing a catastrophic food shortage. So, it is said, they decided to turn a blind eye when a few local families started to farm part of the collectivized land for themselves. They chose not to notice.

What they were soon unable to avoid noticing was that where families were able to farm their own plots of land, and keep the proceeds, productivity shot up. What an intrepid – or perhaps simply desperate – group of farmers had started to do on their own initiative, officials started to encourage elsewhere. Collectivization was quietly scrapped in favour of family-run farms.

Soon, officials were permitting not only the private production of food but allowing farmers to sell the things they produced. The supply of food increased dramatically. By the time the president, Deng Xiaoping, formally allowed family farms, he was simply recognizing what had become a reality for many on the ground.

Others say that the big change in China came about as an unintended consequence of the Cultural Revolution. So traumatized was China's bureaucratic class by this upheaval in the late 1960s and early 1970s, it was no longer up to issuing instructions to every state-owned enterprise from on high. So, some started to take the initiative locally.

Others imply it was all about power politics at the top, and the Chinese leadership was simply looking to repudiate the so-called Gang of Four after Mao's death. The Gang of Four favoured top-down control, so their opponents promoted the opposite. However it came about, there was a profound change in the way that China was run in the late 1970s and early 1980s. The centre stopped trying to run everything – and there followed the most extraordinary growth.

To be clear, China's rulers might have allowed, encouraged even, a decentralization of economic decision-making to provinces and individuals. But there has not been a significant relaxation of political control. As the protesters in Tiananmen Square discovered in 1989, the regime remains intolerant of political dissent. The land might have been decollectivized and the free market enthusiastically embraced, but there is no free market of opinion allowed in China.

As well as decentralising economic decision-making, China began to open up to the outside world. Having felt threatened by hostile powers, China in the decades after the Second World War had shut herself off from the outside world. Gradually, however, she relented. From the 1980s, her rulers encouraged outside investment. Companies from Japan, Germany, America and elsewhere were allowed to set up operations in China. At first, this meant outsiders making things in China. But as know-how and capital flowed into the country, Chinese firms started to produce as part of a global supply chain, too.

China today consumes about half of the world's coal and iron ore produced. In a generation, she has gone from being a country where people used bicycles to get around, to the world's largest consumer – and producer – of cars. Last year, some 17 million cars were sold in China, almost double the number sold just ten years before.

Only three decades ago, China's economy was largely agricultural. In the past few years, it has spawned digital giants like Ten Cent, Ali Baba and Weibo. In 1978, the average Chinese person earned the equivalent of US$155. Last year, the average Chinese income was over US$13,000.

Power was never centralized in India like it had been in China. Decision-making was always dispersed between state and local governments – often chaotically so. What changed in the 1980s is that Indian administrations stopped trying to run the economy. Restrictions on imports were lifted; permits were scrapped. Capital and technology started to flow in, often channelled through India's diaspora. Output started to increase dramatically in the 1990s.

Where China led in the 1980s, and India followed in the 1990s, Indonesia went in the noughties. She opened up, and foreign direct investment flowed in. Exports have subsequently surged. Between 2000 and 2018, according to the World Bank, Indonesia's total annual output increased almost five-fold. The percentage of Indonesians living in poverty has plummeted, from about a quarter of the population twenty years ago to one in ten today.

In 1978, China had a per-capita income and output

similar to a country like Zambia. Since then, Chinese economic output has expanded at about 10 per cent a year – for almost forty years. But now, too, it seems that Zambia and other Sub-Saharan countries are following a similar path towards progress. Per-capita income and output in Africa have more than doubled since 2000, after decades of hardly changing at all.

Across Africa, dictatorship has given way to autocracy. Autocrats have been replaced by elected leaders. Most African rulers today hold office by virtue of some sort of election, however imperfect, rather than an armed coup. Digital technology has opened up Africa so that previously remote farmers are able to buy and sell more freely than ever.

While progress is still in its very early stages, and with very real potential for reversals, it does, however, seem as if Africa south of the Sahara is embarking on a similar journey of rising per-capita incomes and output, and accompanying improvements in living standards.

The conditions conducive to economic take-off have become ubiquitous over the past two hundred years or so. Today, almost every country enjoys independence. However imperfectly, power is more dispersed than it was. Almost every society on earth has greater opportunities to exchange and trade.

Will these benign conditions continue? Is the international order simply sustained by the American superpower?

Being under the Pax Americana ensured that South Korea and Taiwan had the conditions that enabled them to grow. Are we all, in a sense, thriving because of the Pax Americana? Or is it underpinned by some sort of global acceptance of insights about self-order?

PART VI

NEW THREATS TO
FREE SOCIETIES

19

ALTERNATIVE MODELS EMERGE?

Back in the early 1970s, the leaders of the world's leading industrial countries – the United States, Germany, Japan, France, Britain, Canada and Italy – started to hold an annual get-together. This gathering came to be known as the Group of Seven meeting, or just the G7.

Back then, the G7 countries collectively accounted for the lion's share of global output. They still do today. But they are not quite in a league of their own anymore.

Already Italy and Canada have fallen out of the list of the world's seven largest economies. If one was to issue invitations to the leaders of the seven biggest economies today, instead of Italy or Canada, one would need to include the Prime Minister of India – which has now overtaken France – and the President of China – which sits second only to the US.

To avoid having to uninvite anyone, however, the organizers of the G7 added to the guest list, extending invitations to the leaders of the twenty biggest economies instead. The new G20 includes countries such as Turkey, Argentina, Indonesia and Saudi Arabia, too.

But if those on the original guest list such as Italy, Canada, Britain and France are still going to attend in 2040, the organizers will need to make it the G30, or possibly even the G40. Some of those that were leading economies in terms of output within living memory will soon just be pretty average.

Forty years ago, Western states combined accounted for over 60 per cent of world output. Today, it's less than half. By 2040, it will be about a third. A massive pull of plant and capital is underway towards economies that a few decades back could barely feed themselves. It's almost as if we are reverting back to the way things were before the nineteenth century, when the biggest share of world economic activity happened in China, India and elsewhere, rather than in Europe and north America.

Perhaps we should no longer assume that what we call Western liberal democracies are intrinsically more conducive to economic growth and innovation than other parts of the planet. Might it be that there are alternative models emerging that do exchange and innovation better?

ECONOMIC AND DEMOGRAPHIC CHANGE

That the rest of the world is catching up is no bad thing. In fact, it's very good. It's one of the reasons why the world is getting better.

Britain might today only account for 2 per cent or so of global economic output, rather than our 4 or 5 per cent share a generation ago, but unless you are a mercantilist or a madman, why is that a problem? Our relative unimportance might dent the *amour-propre* of the kind of officials who attend G7 summits, but the rest of us are no worse off. Quite the opposite, in fact. India's output is expected to eclipse ours within a few years. Yet we will be much better off in a world in which there are hundreds of millions of middle-class Indians able to afford the things we produce.

The world is not only seeing a shift in the centre of economic gravity. Global demographics are undergoing a profound change, too. The populations of China and India continue to increase, even if the rate of growth is slowing. But it is other parts of the planet where the numbers are rising very rapidly indeed. In 1980, there were about 30 million Ethiopians. Today there are almost three times as many. By 2040, there are expected to be about 164 million. Almost a quarter of a billion people now live in Indonesia. Within twenty years or so, there will be an additional 50 million.

Saudi Arabia had a population of nine million in 1980. In twenty years, there are projected to be over 43 million Saudis. Yemen, which not so very long ago had a population the size of New Zealand, will – according to some estimates – be home to 60 million by 2050. Countries like Tanzania, which a couple of generations ago had a population about the size of Switzerland, are projected to have over 100 million people within a generation or two.* The population of Tanzania's largest city, Dar es Salaam, alone, according to some estimates, will have a bigger population than the whole of France by 2100.†

Of course, we should treat such forecasts with scepticism. Birth rates can fall far faster than experts expect. But even if these demographic growth rates are only half right, there will be an awful lot more people living in Africa, Asia and the Middle East in a generation or so, relative to the numbers in Europe and north America – even with large-scale immigration from the former to the latter.

What might life be like for those living within some of the super-large cities of the future such as Lagos (population estimated at 40 million by 2050), Karachi

* See the website populationpyramid.net for more details of future demographic projections.
† See report by the Global Cities Institute, paper number 4, by Daniel Hoornweg & Kevin Pope, January 2014.

(estimated at 30 million) or Kinshasa (estimated at 35 million)?*

Will those living in these teeming cities enjoy a higher standard of living than they do today, and possibly even a higher one than we in the West currently have? Or will these places become super-slums?

Perhaps you find the idea that someone in Karachi or Lagos might one day have a higher living standard than you in the rich West enjoy today hard to imagine. But ask yourself what someone in eighteenth-century England or America might have thought of the idea that London or New York might one day be home to six or seven million? They would, no doubt, have assumed that any city of such a size would be a scene of gargantuan squalor. They would have found it hard to envisage that a city of such size could be anything other than a bigger version of what was there already.

That is not, of course, how things have turned out. Those living today in London and New York have a vastly better living standard than when such cities were settlements only a fraction of their current size. Indeed, they are rich precisely because of the size and density of their surroundings.

What is going to determine future living standards in

* See report by the Global Cities Institute, paper number 4, by Daniel Hoornweg & Kevin Pope, January 2014.

not just Lagos but London and Manhattan as much as Mumbai, is not the total number of people living in each city, but whether or not specialization and exchange are able to continue to expand the output per person. How likely is this to happen?

For many years, it was commonplace among the educated elites in Britain, America and Europe to see the non-Western world as just a poorer, less developed version of themselves. Given enough time and condescension, these less happy people would in time end up like them. If anything, however, we are seeing signs that some of the emerging economies are developing in a different direction to our own.

AUTOCRATIC ALTERNATIVES

What if some of the fast-growing economies are not just catching up but instead offer an alternative model for growth?

Look at the recent achievement of, say China or Ethiopia. Economic output since the start of this century is up over 400 per cent in China and almost 300 per cent in Ethiopia. Yet neither is in any sense a liberal democracy.

China is a one-party state controlled by the Communist Party. Ethiopia might have many of the trappings of a democracy, but is in reality an autocracy where the government does not tolerate dissent and democracy exists under license.

Democracy *per se* has never been a prerequisite for progress. What counts is constraint upon the powerful, and democracy is just one way of doing it. Throughout history, other influences – other forms of constitutional constraint, or simple geography – have had the same effect.

Countries like China and Ethiopia certainly don't have much democracy to constrain their rulers. But within these states there is an openness to specialization and exchange. Outsiders have been encouraged to invest. Regulation has been reasonable and administered in a way that enables outside businesses to do business. Trade, particularly using digital channels, has taken off. Might there, therefore, be some sort of economically-free/politically-restrained alternative in such states that works better at expanding output per person than our Western way of doing it?

A generation ago, the Soviet system was seen by many as precisely that. The Soviets undoubtedly achieved some extraordinary increases in GDP. Partly this was an inevitable consequence of switching from a predominantly agricultural economy to an industrial one.

Far from being a credible alternative model, however, the output that the Soviet system engineered by command and control was not matched by any corresponding demand – meaning that Russians ended up with too many tractors and too few consumer goods. Without a system of specialization and exchange to allocate resources, growth stalled after the initial advances. In time, the Soviet model provided a good example of how not to develop.

A lot of the growth we have seen so far in China, Ethiopia or Indonesia is due to large injections of capital meeting with large numbers of people. As the rural population floods into cities, and moves from agriculture to industry, output per person leaps ahead. Whether these increases are sustainable depends on the extent to which specialization and exchange are allowed to continue. None of these states, of course, comes even close to the Soviet system in terms of having a command and control economy. Quite the opposite, in fact. Inward flows of investment are allowed, together with a relatively benign regulatory environment.

But what are the chances that in time, those with power in Beijing, Addis Ababa or Jakarta, like those in Putin's Moscow, get in the way of free exchange? Relying on the self-restraint of those with political power is unlikely to be enough.

LIMITS OF AUTOCRACY

After the Soviet system failed, Russia, it was often said, would move towards the Western model. Elections were held and the economy apparently liberalized. Yet we now know that after a period of chaos, Russia has in reality headed off in a very different direction.

Turkey, too, was supposed to have 'Westernized'. Under Atatürk, she threw out her old alphabet, as well as all sorts of antiquated ways. She was a democracy for more years in the last century than Germany. Yet today she seems to be heading back towards something more traditional – Ottoman perhaps, rather than tsarist. Following an apparent coup attempt in 2016, thousands of the government's critics have been locked up. Having interfered in civil society, Turkey's Islamist political elite are starting to intervene in the workings of the free economy.

China has never made any pretence of being a democracy. Yet for much of the past forty years, she certainly seemed to be liberalizing. Deng Xiaoping's reforms of the early 1980s meant a new constitution, preventing any one person or faction from holding too much power for too long. Autonomy was granted to maritime provinces, and special economic zones were created as places of innovation and experimentation.

Yet since 2012 China seems to have taken a different trajectory. President Xi did away with Deng's term limits, making himself a leader for life. He has cultivated a personality cult not seen since Mao. Deng's reforms seem to be unravelling. Beijing's bureaucracy is becoming much more involved and intrusive. The authorities have created a new range of restrictions on China's digital economy, making firms seek permission for all sorts of things – and then withholding permission apparently arbitrarily.

A long and growing list of outside internet firms have been banned from China, including Google, Facebook, YouTube, Netflix, WhatsApp and many others. Some might see in this an ulterior motive – economic nationalism. Keeping out US digital giants, they imply, is a way of ensuring that a Chinese alternative emerges. Maybe. Or maybe it's the twenty-first-century version of banning the printing press.

China's own digital firms, such as Ten Cent, have suffered at the hands of arbitrary rule-making, having various regulatory permissions revoked without warning. It is the sort of behaviour that one might have expected to see if China was still ruled by the Ming. And if a society is ruled by those that behave like the Ming, imposing restrictive rules on everything, it will share the fate of sixteenth-century China. Stagnation will set in, followed by decline. History is littered with states that showed precocious promise without going on to achieve sustained progress.

If Turkey's President Erdoğan and his successors re-create a twenty-first-century version of the old Ottoman sultanate, Turkey will suffer the sort of stagnation she experienced in that earlier age. She will become like Russia, whose leader behaves like a modern tsar, and whose economy is now smaller in size than the economy of Texas or Spain.

Democracy does not necessarily produce 'better' leaders. Often it patently doesn't. For every great President, Prime Minister or Consul that democracy has produced, it has also delivered plenty of duds. For every Lincoln, Churchill or Scipio Africanus, there have been all too many Richard Nixons and Lyndon Johnsons – charlatans at worst, mediocrities at best.

A technocracy tends to install in high office those who, on paper and in theory anyway, are better qualified to decide. But that's the point. They might be better qualified to decide – *and with that comes a presumption that they should decide*. In a democracy – where the *demos* are the ultimate arbiters – there is a greater chance that the natural inclination of elites to try to decide things will be kept in check. That means there is more space for the possibility that human social and economic affairs might be left to order themselves.

The really important point about democracy is not that it creates institutional constraint, but constraints on the moral authority of elites to act and intervene. It is impossible to be quite so hands-on in trying to order the affairs of the masses when the masses have a say over what happens.

Electorates are unpredictable. Mandates are necessarily time limited. Experts who would rather make public policy without the inconvenience of an electoral cycle have to contend with what ordinary folk might make of it all. Voters might well make a 'wrong' decision. And it is in that very notion of 'wrongness' – people not conforming with some small elite's idea of what shape society ought to take – that the real significance of democracy sits. Democracy means that there is a much greater chance that social and economic affairs will be able to order themselves, and this being so, be much more prone to progress.

We do not know if what we are seeing is a temporary blip among some of the emerging economies, like Turkey and China, or if these countries are now heading off on a decidedly more *dirigiste* direction. What we can be sure of is that if they do become less open to exchange and innovation – even if they do not necessarily veer off towards greater autocracy – this reduced openness will in the longer term ensure that these states become less successful.

TURNING JAPANESE

Thirty years ago, many American politicians were obsessed about Japan, seeing it as a threat.

Given open access to US markets after the Second World War, Japan enjoyed remarkable economic growth in the 1950s, 1960s and 1970s. So much so, in fact, that in one sector after another – ball bearings, machine tools, cameras, ship-building, semiconductors and electronics – Japanese companies started to dominate the market place. Between 1960 and 1980, Japan's share of world car production rose from 1 per cent to 23 per cent.

With Japanese exports flooding overseas markets, earnings poured back. Japan then started to invest her new wealth by buying up American businesses, including iconic companies such as Hollywood's Columbia Pictures. Her banks established enormous property portfolios across US cities.

All this would lead, some feared, to Japanese hegemony. A book even appeared on the *New York Times* bestseller list predicting a coming war with an aggressive, militaristic Japan.* Some even suggested that Japan was such a regimented society she was almost some kind of new Spartan state.

Of course, none of that came to pass. Japan remains a democracy. She has also really struggled economically. The Japanese model that everyone once went on about turned out not to be such a great way to innovate and grow after all. Far from eclipsing America, Japan's economy has flatlined since the early 1990s. Japanese household income per person in 2017 is what it was in 2000. To try to lift her out of her economic funk, successive Japanese

---

* See, for example, *The Coming War with Japan* by George Friedman and Meredith Lebard (1991).

governments have spent so much money that they have managed to accumulate the highest level of public debt to GDP in the world.

Japan led the world when the Sony Walkman was at the cutting edge of consumer technology. But since then Japan has missed out on a lot of digital innovation altogether. She has produced few notable digital giants. Her economy, dominated by giant cartel-forming companies, has produced few innovators or innovations. To grasp the extent of her slow-down, try to imagine for a moment that America today had only IBM, and no Apple. Or that Oracle was her leading information provider, not Google.

Japan shows us that we should not assume that an economy will continue to grow rapidly just because it did in the past. If specialization and exchange is in any way inhibited, growth and innovation slow down, no matter how much your economy might have advanced before.

Post-war Japan grew as a large post-war population entered the labour market, alongside a massive injection of capital. But with that massive injection of capital came a massive misallocation of credit. Dud investments were not allowed to fail. A lot of bad debts grew. Asset prices were chronically over-inflated by the late 1980s.

Japanese growth was all about exports, making much of her output contingent on meeting overseas demand, not necessarily a domestic one. The Japanese model that emerged also meant having a few very large producers in each sector. This, of course, was great for export growth, with all kinds of efficiencies and economies of scale made possible. But an approach that was good at gaining overseas market share was not so great at enabling innovation and new entrants. Large Japanese conglomerates acquired cosy relations with officialdom. A kind of crony corporatism emerged.

Japan's economy has slowed for all sorts of reasons. But the fact that her economy is dominated by large conglomerates – many of whom are export-dependent, able to keep out any competition, and up to their eyeballs in debt – is a large part of the problem. No amount of government spending can compensate for it and make Japan dynamic again.

It's no longer Japan that is spoken of as a strategic threat to America, but China instead. She is seen as some sort of new Sparta. Indeed, there is even talk in Washington of America and China supposedly being stuck in a 'Thucydides trap' – a reference to the way that Sparta and Athens were seemingly unable to avoid conflict, as one waxed while the other waned.

Maybe. We cannot know for sure what the future holds. But we should not repeat the error of assuming that China is inexorably set on a path of ascendency. Her economic dynamism is ultimately a function of how open she is to innovation and exchange. And she, too, may be about to turn a bit more Japanese than she might like.

Within China, some very large export-oriented corporations have emerged with close, symbiotic relationships with officialdom. In China, too, a kind of crony corporatism is emerging. It is not always clear where big business ends and officialdom begins. Rather like Japan in the late 1980s, there is a lot of bad debt in China, as well as some seriously over-inflated asset prices. China, and some of the other emerging economies, could be a credit cycle or so away from turning Japanese. The Xi era system of top-down controls and more arbitrary rule-making will, in time, mean less dynamism and growth.

But then again, maybe it's not just China that has begun to turn a little Japanese. Perhaps we in the West have, too? There is an awful lot of bad debt and crony capitalism in Europe and America as well.

When pundits talk of there being alternatives to the Western Model, what they usually mean is some sort of non-Western way of doing things emerging elsewhere in the world. But what if the alternative model to emerge is within the West itself?

Could it be that the West has changed, incrementally, undeclared and almost imperceptibly, towards a very different kind of political economy over the past few decades? Perhaps the threat to free societies comes not from a Sparta on the outside, but the corruption of the Athens from within.

20

THE RISE OF THE TECHNOCRATIC STATE

Across Europe and America have emerged pan-continental federations over the past forty years, presided over by bureaucratic forms of government, increasingly remote from the people. Power that was once dispersed across European Union member states or US states of the union increasingly resides within technocratic institutions in Brussels and Washington.

There has been a profound change to the political economy of the West, with democracy giving way to technocracy. Quite apart from the political implications, this is already starting to have big consequences for free exchange. In Europe in particular, and to a growing extent in America, the production, purchase, sale and consumption of almost all goods and services involves some sort of oversight, approval, permission-granting and control by some or other branch of government. Europe – and to a less degree America – are becoming less open and free and steadily more sclerotic.

THE URGE TO INTERVENE

In nineteenth-century Britain and America government tended to be small, intervention limited and bureaucracy minimal. In the last two decades of the nineteenth century, however, some began to argue that government ought to do more.

It was the example of Germany, we are often told, that prompted pressure for a more interventionist form of government. Recently unified, Germany was such a success story, apparently, that she was held up as the alternative model of the day, to be envied and emulated. By the 1890s, Germany had overtaken Britain by many measures. This had a profound effect on England, we are told, almost shaking her out of her Victorian sense of superiority. Germany was not so far behind the United States, either.

Across the English-speaking world, many began to ask if the German way of doing things, with the state orchestrating from above, might be better. Perhaps the mid-Victorian idea of a minimalist state was redundant?

What was happening in Germany certainly influenced a number of American observers, such as for example, Woodrow Wilson, still at the time a mere professor at Princeton University. Like others, Wilson argued that public administration in America, as in Germany, needed to be entrusted to experts, unconstrained by popular consent. America might have been given a form of government by her Founding Fathers as an agrarian republic, but that was unequal to the new task of 'scientific administration'. What was needed, according to the Progressive movement that emerged in early-twentieth-century America, was a new 'fourth branch of government'.

The problem for the Progressives was that the Constitution made no provision for any new branch of government. According to the Supreme Court at the time, it was not permissible for Congress to delegate to others their authority to make laws.

This kind of constitutional constraint proved initially pretty effective. The ambition to increase the shape and scope of government might have been there, but the Constitution thwarted the growth of government – at least initially. Once Professor Wilson was in the White House, he managed to create a Federal Reserve Bank. Progressives even managed to amend the Constitution to allow a federal income tax to be collected for the first time. When mobilizing for the First World War, the federal administration might have managed to start planning and directing the economy in all sorts of new ways. But it was not until the 1930s that big government got its big break.

THE NEW DEAL AND AFTER

It was the Great Depression that enabled many of the constitutional constraints that had frustrated an earlier generation of Progressives to be set aside. Faced with a massive fall in output between 1929 and when he took office in 1932, America's new president, Franklin Roosevelt, managed to establish a vast alphabet soup of federal agencies – from the AAA (Agricultural Adjustment Administration) to the CWA (Civil Works Administration) and the WPA (Works Progress Administration). Under the New Deal, the federal government created a system of centralized planning, run by the National Recovery Administration, to spur industrial production.

In order to put in place the apparatus of a regulatory state, Roosevelt had to concentrate power in the hands of the executive, and various new executive agencies. Previously, Congress had been required to approve the spending of any executive offices. Instead, Roosevelt, having created dozens of new executive offices, granted himself the power to allocate them their vast budget by executive order. At one time, he even threatened to pack the Supreme Court with new, sympathetic judges to avoid having the judiciary frustrate his efforts to empower this new form of executive administration.

Something rather similar happened in Britain at about the same time. The House of Commons, even more so than Congress, lost much of its meaningful control over public spending. In the 1930s, well before the outbreak of the Second World War, the Standing Orders of the House of Commons were changed so that MPs were no longer able to control how funds were allocated within overall spending estimates.

Well before the outbreak of the Second World War, we can see significant changes that allowed the expansion of public administration into areas of social and economic life where previously no official would have got involved. But where did this urge to intervene come from?

The drive towards bigger government, according to conventional accounts, came either from a desire to emulate Germany in the late nineteenth century, or else it came from the need to defeat her in the twentieth century. Or at other times we are told it was born out of necessity, when the economy slumped in the 1930s.

The New Deal and World War might help explain how government grew big, but neither properly explains why it was that people wanted to create a much more proactive system of public administration in the first place. Nor does what happened in the 1930s and 1940s do much to explain why some of the really big expansions in the role of the state have happened over the past forty years.

In 1960, when the Second World War was already a memory, government spending in most European countries was about a third of GDP. In France it was a little more, at 34 per cent. In Sweden a little less, at 31 per cent. In the United States it was slightly lower still, at 27 per cent.

Half a century on, government spending in each of those countries had increased very significantly; it is now about 44 per cent in Germany, and not far off half of GDP in Britain and Sweden. The state spends almost 60 per cent of GDP each year in France. Even in America, government spending is now at a level – 37 per cent – that would have seemed positively un-American to many a few decades ago.

In Britain today, a hodgepodge of government agencies exists, many known by their acronyms – among them ACE (or the Arts Council England), BFEG (the Biometrics and Forensic Ethics Group), CQC (the Care Quality Commission) and the DWI (the Drinking Water Inspectorate). In fact, there are so many such bureaucratic configurations that we seem to have run out of enough acronyms to name them all, with at least two FSAs (a Food

Standards Agency and a Financial Services Authority). In America, there's a DHS and DHHS, one presiding over homeland security, the other over health and science. Then there's a HUD and an HRU, and several hundred other agencies deciding public policy.

Over the past three or four decades, government has become so big it has outgrown conventional governance constraints. The various legislatures simply cannot keep track of all the decisions being made by every branch of government and bureaucracy. In Britain, not even ministers are aware of all the public policy-making going on in their own departments.

To properly appreciate why liberal states have become so much more technocratic over the past generation or so, it's necessary to look not at what happened in the 1930s and 1940s, but to understand a change that has occurred in the nature of liberalism itself.

THE CORRUPTION OF LIBERALISM

The word 'liberal' comes from the Latin *liber*, meaning free. *Liber*-al used to carry strong connotations of self-direction. A *liber*-al society was one that was not ordered from above, and a *liber*-al economy shaped itself, rather than being shaped by blueprint.

This old idea of liberalism had its roots in empiricism

and the scientific discoveries of the eighteenth and nineteenth centuries. Science had revealed much about the self-ordering nature of the world around us. A liberal thus knew that progress and order – in the human world, as well as the natural world – did not need direction from above. A liberal was an empiricist who rejected the idea of authority in regard to knowledge. In his famous essay 'On Liberty', John Stuart Mill (1806–73) went out of his way to emphasize that none of us can claim intellectual infallibility. As Richard Feynman said of scientists, an old-school liberal 'believed in the ignorance of experts'.

Far from believing in the ignorance of experts, social scientists today believe in their infallibility. Rather than empiricism, they take what David Deutsch has described as an 'inductivist' approach. A theory about the economy or society is formed. Observations are then made to try to find facts that fit the theory.*

Inductivism is not quite the same as uber-rationalism – a belief that it is possible to come to conclusions without empirical observations about the world. But it is a belief that such observations can be selectively presented to support a certain set of conclusions. This is why so often inductivists end up fitting evidence around

---

* See Deutsch, D., *The Fabric of Reality: The Science of Parallel Universes and Its Implications* (1997) for more on this point.

a favoured theory, and calling it 'evidence-based policy-making'. It is a form of confirmation bias, and it under-lies the approach of many public policy-makers in Britain, Europe and America.

Old-school liberals avoided placing much faith in grand plans. Theories as to how to order human affairs were treated with scepticism, and certainly not validated merely because of the weight of expert opinion behind them. The process of peer-reviewing academic papers, widespread within university humanities departments these days, is a process of validation that relies almost exclusively on the weight of expert opinion.

The confirmation-bias approach of policy-makers encourages group-think as well as overconfidence. It allows policy-makers to overestimate their ability to understand the world and inordinately complex economic or social systems within it. This has egged on the expansion of public administration.

Empiricism once curbed the claims of small elites to be able to order society by design. Inductivism has returned us to the idea that a small elite has authority over knowledge. It has given them an inflated ambition as to how they might engineer certain social and economic outcomes.

This explains why a 'liberal', in the contemporary American sense of the term, is not someone that recognizes the importance of self-order at all. Far from it; a liberal tends to believe that it is not only possible to engineer certain social and economic outcomes, but that without doing so any society will be somehow sub-optimal.

Not surprisingly perhaps, the longer people are marinaded in these ideas in their university humanities departments, the more inclined they are to hold faith in experts. And, perhaps one might add, the less tolerant many seem to be of those who may think otherwise. From this the urge to intervene has increased.

If a bogus empiricism has corrupted liberalism through conceit, giving small elites a greater urge to intervene, a change made in the way that governments manage money handed them the means to do so with little constraint.

THE MEANS TO EXPAND: THE NIXON SHOCK

Richard Nixon has gone down in history as a bad American president. And rightly so. His name will be forever associated with the Watergate scandal, when his cronies broke into the Democratic Party headquarters in Washington. But sanctioning a burglary was not the worst decision he made in the Oval Office.

Watergate might have made Nixon a crook, but it was his decision to break the link between the dollar and gold on 15 August 1971 that enabled the growth of big government. By breaking that link, he also broke a fundamental fiscal constraint on government.

The most effective constraint on the size of government is the link between taxation and representation. The American revolutionaries understood this, which is why they famously insisted that there be 'no taxation without representation'. As long as taxpayers were represented, and as long as taxpayers were expected to pay for any increase in government spending, there would always be pressure to keep government limited. No matter how successful Wilson, Roosevelt and all the others were at overturning various constitutional constraints, if the taxpayers had to pay for it all, there was a limit to the size of the federal bureaucracy that could be created. But what Nixon did was to break the link between taxation and representation, so that governments could spend without taxation on a vast scale.

Often presented as a minor tweak ending an outdated monetary relic from the past, or as a pragmatic response to the inflationary pressures that came with fighting the Vietnam War, Nixon's decision was what made possible the subsequent emergence of the technocratic state.

Before August 1971, the US dollar was pegged to gold at the rate of US$35 per ounce, under what was called the Bretton Woods System. Under this international agreement, the American government was committed to backing every dollar overseas with gold. Crucially, this meant that the quantity of US dollars that the US government could put into circulation was limited by the amount of gold that the US government had.* So many additional dollars have been created since then that an ounce of gold today is worth more than US$1,315.

The 'Nixon shock' meant that the US government unilaterally cancelled the convertibility of the United States dollar to gold. From then on, the United States government could borrow enormous amounts to finance deficit spending. With the US dollar now a fiat currency, it was just a paper promise and the US government could make a great many of those. Doing so enabled the US government to keep funding the Vietnam War. Nixon's successors have been funding deficits to pay for all sorts of things ever since.

To be sure, governments have been able to borrow to cover any shortfall between tax revenue and spending for centuries. In the sixteenth century, for example, the

---

* To be sure, Bretton Woods was already creaking before Nixon made his announcement. Immediately beforehand, there was a run on US gold reserves, with foreign governments converting the dollars they held into gold. But this was itself a consequence of the US government increasing the money supply too fast. Under Bretton Woods the dollar was convertible to gold at a fixed rate (for foreign governments, not individuals). This meant that if the Federal Reserve increased the money supply, inflating the dollar, the real value of the dollar fell but the nominal price in gold did not. Naturally, other countries then swapped their dollars for gold, causing the gold run. Incidentally, this also explains why West Germany felt the need to leave the Bretton Woods System in April 1971.

Dutch and English issued bonds to help them wage war. What changed once the US dollar became merely a paper promise is the sheer scale of borrowing. After 1971, the only thing that constrained the amount of money in the economy was government. In other words, government was no longer effectively constrained at all.

Setting a currency 'free' sounds uplifting. But if it isn't bound to something external with independent worth, why should it retain its value? By the end of the 1970s, the US dollar had depreciated by a third. Inflation in America surged to 12 per cent in the immediate aftermath of the Nixon shock. In Britain, it reached 24 per cent by 1975. It remained persistently high on either side of the Atlantic for a decade after the presidential announcement.

America, of course, wasn't the only country affected. Under Bretton Woods, most Western currencies were indirectly tied to gold by their peg to the dollar. Once the dollar's link to gold was broken, currencies in most Western states became fiat money – mere paper promises. This meant that from August 1971 onwards, not just the US government, but governments in the UK, France, Japan and elsewhere could make as many paper promises as they pleased. And that, to put it crudely, is what they did.

France last balanced the books in 1974, three years after the Nixon shock. The UK government has only managed to avoid a deficit in eight years since that time. In America, since 1971 deficit spending has become the norm in peace time in a way that it never was before. Since 2001 the national debt in America doubled from US$6 trillion to US$12 trillion by 2009 – and is projected to double again to US$24 trillion by the mid-2020s.

The really big, sustained increase in the size of US government happened not during the First or Second World Wars, but in the decades since 1971. Many Western states had different sorts of welfare provision long before the 1970s, but it is really only since the early 1970s that the vast network of redistributive programmes, through which government transfers wealth from one section of society to another, sprung up.

THE MEANS TO EXPAND:
A SUPRANATIONAL UNION

In America, an increasingly technocratic system of government arose as the old constitutional constraints were side-stepped. In Europe, a pan-continental federation was created not by changing the nature of any existing system of government but by establishing an entirely new one. A series of supranational institutions were put in place which were, by their very nature, above much meaningful public accountability from the outset.

Under a succession of treaties – Rome 1957, Maastricht 1992, Amsterdam 1997, Nice 2001, Lisbon 2007 – the member states of what we now call the European Union delegated decision-making to a new set of pan-European institutions.

From 1958, a European Commission came into existence, which was to have the power to make binding regulations that took precedence over any national law. In the half century that has followed, the Commission has taken to producing each year a blizzard of rules governing many aspects of economic activity and social policy. Often introduced under the auspices of encouraging trade across Europe, the point has long been passed when it can be pretended that such rule-making is about facilitating intra-EU trade.

A European Court in Strasbourg is the highest judicial authority within the EU and polices the system, all the while being mandated to rule in favour of 'ever closer union'. It also enforces the doctrine of *acquis communautaire*, whereby an area of public policy that has been delegated to an EU institution is seen to have been ceded to them by the member states irrevocably. As you might imagine, this has resulted in a concentration of power.

A European Central Bank manages the currency of those member states that have ditched their own currencies in favour of a common currency, the Euro. The

ECB sets interest rates and determines monetary policy on behalf of about 400 million EU citizens. Meanwhile, a series of federal EU agencies have enormous administrative power and are able to approve everything from new medicines to member states' budgets.

As in the United States, once various constitutional innovations had enabled Roosevelt and his successors to create what was in effect an entirely new branch of government, the European Union has bequeathed to public officials in Europe the administrative means to order the affairs of an entire continent from on high. In the United States, the Nixon shock also delivered the financial means to fund all this extra government. In Europe, too, pan-Europe institutions have had money allocated to them with only the most cursory accountability to any taxpayers. The European Union's own Court of Auditors has, infamously, refused to sign-off on the EU's accounts in almost twenty years.

While in America the power of federal authorities has increased, they do not have quite the freedom that federal agencies have in Europe. Congress is still able to veto spending and even bring the whole federal bureaucracy to a standstill. No European parliament possesses such powers, or any sort of inclination to use them.

Those that run various federal agencies in America are still appointed by those that Americans elect. The EU agencies are staffed by a cadre of officials immune to any sort of accountability. The Supreme Court of the United States, for all its apparent failings and controversies, still rules on the basis of what the Constitution says. Unlike the European Court, it is not in the business of agglomerating power at the federal level as an objective in itself.

In Europe, even more so than in America, the idea that there is a Western model of limited government with free and open markets, is starting to seem a little dated. There is a technocratic state instead. And this is beginning to have all kinds of implications for economic expansion and innovation.

NEW MODEL, SLOWER GROWTH

Since 2009, output in China has increased by 139 per cent. In India, by 96 per cent. Even in the United States, output is up a very healthy 34 per cent. In Europe? Output in the Eurozone has fallen by 2 per cent.

Yet Europe was, within living memory, one of the fastest growing places on the planet. In the 1950s and 1960s, output increased on average at 5.5 per cent a year – faster than anywhere else, apart from Japan. Economic indices showed Europe and Japan each becoming relatively more – not less – important in world economic affairs.

Then, about thirty or forty years ago something in

Europe changed. Growth started to slow. Between 1950 and 1973, average output per person in Europe rose 4 per cent a year. Since 1973, the rate of increase has almost halved. Decline is no longer merely relative but by some measures absolute.

To be sure, slower economic growth as the post-war period of reconstruction came to an end was in some ways unavoidable. The easy gains in output that come from rebuilding bombed-out cities and factories – financed in part by American Marshall Aid – ran their course. But there was more to it than that. What also happened is that Europe became less open to free exchange.

When we think of new, emerging economies catching up economically, there is an implicit assumption that after an initial burst of growth, they will slow down as they mature. A little like post-war Europe, the early gains in output per person don't last long, as a country moves from agricultural to industrial production, or simply urbanizes. But beyond that, why do we assume that a highly specialized 'mature' economy must necessarily slow down?

Surely what we know about specialization and exchange tells us that the more interconnected things become, the more growth and innovation ought to accelerate, no? Far from growing weary with age like a body, a 'mature' economy has a greater capacity for specialization and exchange, allocating resources evermore effectively and increasing innovation exponentially?

Yet instead Europe has done the opposite. She has slowed down compared not only to emerging economies, but to other advanced economies. As output in Europe fell in absolute terms after 2009, in America it went up by over a third, in Australia by about 60 per cent and in Canada by over 30 per cent.

To be fair, America and the other Western states at times also show symptoms of the same ailment. When you look at per-capita increases in output, the US picture is not as impressive as the raw GDP data suggests. She, too, is less open to innovation and exchange than she was. In the 1960s, US GDP increased at an average rate of over 4 per cent a year. By the noughties, annual output was increasing at less than half that rate.

The more pronounced the emergence of technocracy, the more evident the economic slowdown. Over the past three decades in Europe, as a rough rule of thumb, those parts of the continent furthest removed from the technocratic EU state have generally performed best; Switzerland and Norway, outside the EU, have outperformed Britain or Italy, inside. Britain, which had certain opt-outs from the EU even before the Brexit vote, has increased output faster than Germany or France. Turkey, too, has outstripped Greece.

Ironically, many of those things that restrict free exchange in Europe have been introduced in the name of the free market, or at least the EU's Single Market.

Ostensibly about free trade, the Single Market in reality handed enormous power to officials. Instead of enabling goods and services legally produced in one member state to be sold in any other, it ensures that goods and services can only be produced and sold anywhere if they comply with a common set of standards. All too often, common standards are drafted in a way that favours established interests.

Labour laws across Europe restrict labour markets, making European producers less competitive. Regulation of energy markets has increased energy costs in Europe, pricing European companies out of world markets and creating all kinds of incentives for EU-based producers to lobby to restrict access to EU markets to keep out the competition.

From food-processing to car-manufacturing to house-building, multiple agencies determine what producers can sell to customers and on what terms. Regulation is routinely used by vested interests to prevent the emergence of new entrants, even if the price of doing so is less innovation overall. Compliance costs can be imposed to ensure smaller competitors cannot compete.

Despite all the talk about consumer protection, much EU rule-making is done to restrict supply in the interest of established suppliers. This is why big businesses employ armies of lobbyists to help write the rules in Brussels.

Things have reached a stage where in many areas of

economic activity, big producers in Europe do not just use their marketing budgets to try to persuade willing customers to buy their products at a price they are willing to pay. Instead, they put large chunks of their budgets into lobbying regulators to ensure that their customers must buy from them on their terms.

Trade agreements that the EU strikes with third-party countries might use the language of free trade, but they also have a nasty habit of stipulating on what terms trade might take place at all. They extend Single Market-style mercantilism around the world. Far from freeing up trade, the Single Market achieves the opposite. It has killed off innovation and intensive economic growth in Europe. Europe's economy has slowed down notably since 1992 and she has become ever less innovative.

Three decades ago, the twelve countries that then constituted what became the EU registered 25 per cent of global patents. Today, that has fallen to a pitiful 4 per cent. It's not just a case of other parts of the world becoming more innovative. Europe is falling behind with an absolute fall in innovation.

Venice at the start of the seventeenth century was still one of the richest places on the planet. In terms of art and architecture, she was going through a Golden Age. Had you lived there at the time, the trappings of success would have been all around you. And yet Venice had, almost indiscernibly at first, started to slow down. Other parts of the world had started to take her share of the textile market in the eastern Mediterranean. Venice was no longer the undisputed centre for book publishing, either. Nor had she produced any major new technology or other innovation in a couple of centuries or so. Venetian galleys might still have been good for travelling around that inland sea, the Mediterranean, but they weren't up to much on the sort of ocean-going voyages that were starting to have such vital importance.

The idea that Venice might have been losing her top spot because others, like the Dutch or the English, were catching up might have helped console those on the Rialto troubled by such things. But such excuses would have missed the point. Irrespective of how much others might have been speeding up, Venice was starting to slow down. So, too, is Europe today.

Like those distant Venetians, Europe is today relatively prosperous. Living standards are, as a whole, higher than they have ever been, and many of those living in Europe are much better off than many others living in the neighbourhood (which is one of the reasons why, like Venice, so many of the neighbours try to move in each year). But Europe is no longer the centre of the world economy. Venice, which was once the economic hub of the Mediterranean, became just another port city. Europe, once the centre of the world economy, is well on her way to being just another peninsula on the Eurasian land mass.

THE INTERNATIONAL ORDER

In global terms, you might think, none of this really matters. Venice stagnated, so innovation and industry moved elsewhere. Europe today might turn herself into a giant museum, open to outside students and tourists, but others will avoid her mistakes. Humankind overall will progress.

Perhaps. But the same sort of technocratic outlook and institutions that have done so much to hinder innovation and exchange in Europe also underpin much of the non-European international order, too.

Set up after the Second World War, many of the institutions on which the global system of open markets and free trade exist – the United Nations, the World Health Organization, the IMF, World Bank and World Trade Organization – are not immune to the ambitions of small, supranational elites who aspire to shape the world by design and blueprint.

Those who set the agenda within such institutions belong to a tribe that the American political scientist, Samuel Huntington, called 'transnationalists'. They increasingly see 'national boundaries as obstacles that thankfully are vanishing and see national governments as residues from the past whose only useful function is to facilitate the elite global operations'.

The risk is that the move towards technocracy goes

supranational – a sort of EU operating at a global level. Already we have seen in recent years attempts to create supranational courts and institutions. Treaties are signed, under the guise of tackling various global problems, which invariably empower small elites to decide things that were once left to national governments. Our transnationalist elites presume to be in possession of insights and knowledge denied to ordinary mortals or indeed mere governments.

Giving power to unaccountable rule-makers inevitably means you end up with more rules. It's increasingly about ordering international affairs by blueprint and design. The idea of self-order between sovereign states is being steadily eroded.

The essence of liberalism is surely self-government. It is a measure of how illiberal our international order is becoming that it is presided over by a system of supranational decision-making that often seems to treat the idea of national self-determination with contempt.

21

POPULISM

The threat to free societies comes from political populism, apparently. Liberal democracies around the world are under attack from within; Donald Trump in America, an Alternative für Deutschland (AfD) in Germany, Geert Wilders in the Netherlands, Sverige-demokraterna in Sweden and Viktor Orbán in Hungary. And Brexit Britain.

The electoral success of such insurgent forces is ominous for the future of liberal democracy, according to disapproving public intellectuals like Yascha Mounk. The BBC even made a video using Plato's quote about dictatorship arising out of democracy to suggest that Donald Trump in the White House marked the beginning of tyranny in America.*

* BBC Newsnight, January 18, 2017.

Then there is the success of the radical Left. It's no longer a few fringe figures or Venezuelan autocrats speaking the language of redistribution. In America, Kamala Harris and Alexandria Ocasio-Cortez have been elected advocating these sorts of ideas. Across the Western world, traditionally socialist ideas about capitalism and class struggle have been given a toxic new lease of life under the guise of identity politics. Entire groups of people, as defined by their gender or ethnic group, are assigned a role as either one of the exploiters or exploited.

What explains the rise of this political populism? It's all about economic inequality, apparently.

GROWING ECONOMIC
INEQUALITY...

Since the early 1990s, hundreds of millions of workers have been added to the productive base of the world economy. As China and India opened up economically and the Iron Curtain came down, the labour supply within the global trading system trebled in size.

In China alone, over 70 million manufacturing jobs have been created since 2000 – vastly more than the combined total of 42 million manufacturing jobs recorded in the whole of Europe and the United States in 2012.* All that additional cheap labour meant lower median wage growth for Western workers. In America, the real median income of working-age males has only increased by 6 per cent since 1971.† It's why, they say, only 66 per cent of working-age American men today hold full-time jobs – a record low.

At the same time as all that, the digital economy started to have some pretty profound consequences, allowing a tiny number of people to amass great fortunes while destroying lots of blue-collar jobs, apparently.

It's perfectly true that in a digital world, marginal costs are low. That is to say, the cost of producing one app for one single user or producing an app that is downloaded by a million users is not that different. One of the consequences of this is that a preeminent product – whether it's a search engine or taxi app – often won't just have a preeminent slice of the market but will end up dominating it. Digital, it sometimes seems, is made to produce monopolies – or at least ensure that the best become ubiquitous at the expense of anything else.

Compare that to what happens in a non-digital market, such as the car industry. Think of the top-selling family cars. General Motors has 17 per cent of the American

---

*   King, M., *The End of Alchemy* (2016), p. 27.
†   Gilder, G., *The Scandal of Money: Why Wall Street Recovers But the Economy Never Does* (2016), p. 4.

market; Ford has 16 per cent. There is even space in the market for Volkswagen and Mazda with a tiddly 3 and 2 per cent respectively. But what about the digital market? Who uses any search engine besides Google? What was the name of that thing you used to talk to friends online before Facebook? For many, Facebook *is* social media. Uber started out as one of a number of taxi-summoning apps. It has become ubiquitous – not only in New York and London, but in Delhi and Nairobi, too. The winner seems to take everything.

And then there's automation. Artificial Intelligence, according to Feng Xiang, law professor at Tsinghua University, 'will inexorably result in a super-rich oligopoly of data billionaires who reap the wealth created by robots that displace human labour, leading to massive unemployment in their wake'.*

The only trouble with the idea that globalization and automation are driving down living standards and increasing inequality is that it's a myth. Living standards are rising and inequality is not.

... IS A MYTH

Hundreds of millions of additional Chinese, Indian and

---

* Feng Xiang article in the *Washington Post*, May 3rd, 2018.

eastern European workers have joined the global work-force. But at the same time, tens of millions of new jobs have been generated in the West, too. In 1990, there were 109 million Americans in employment. Today there are 144 million. In Britain, the workforce has increased from 27 million to 31 million. Far from mass unemployment, there are more jobs in Britain and America today than ever before – and this great growth spurt in job-creation has coincided with greater global economic interdependence.

Many of the new jobs might be low paid, but globali-zation also means lots of cheap, more affordable con-sumer goods. If globalization has dragged down median wages for blue-collar America and Britain, it has also slashed the cost of living for millions.

Since 1996, the real cost of household appliances has fallen by over 40 per cent; the cost of footwear and clothes by 60 per cent. Previous generations of mums and dads struggling to make ends meet complained about not being able to afford shoes for their kids. Today's parents can buy them from Tesco for five quid. With the real price of TVs and music-players down by 90 per cent, their kids don't just have more shoes, they probably have a TV in their bedroom, too.

If blue-collar Joe Six-pack now earns less due to glo-balization, he is also able to afford an awful lot more from Walmart or Wilko – or perhaps I should say, Amazon – because of it. The lowest price or best deal is now ubiquitous. Like me, you don't even need to be a particularly discerning shopper to benefit from it. Far from driving up inequality, global trade in the age of the internet is a great leveller, and even those on average incomes are able to buy the kind of consumer goods we once considered luxuries.

Those who attack the gig economy and globalization are really attacking the evermore refined and sophisticated division of labour. They ignore the effect that it has on elevating living standards, driving up employment opportunities and making it easier than ever for folk to find work.

Like Rousseau, they insist that the division of labour is demeaning; that the ability of workers to work the shifts they want when they want is exploitation; that the ability of global supply chains to provide us with low-cost food and clothing is somehow undignified. This notion that the division of labour impoverishes us is no truer today than it was when Rousseau was alive.

There is an even more fundamental problem with the 'Globalization + Digital = Inequality' equation: inequality is not increasing. Over the past two decades, we have seen much greater globalization and the take-off of the digital economy. *But if anything, income inequality has actually declined.*

You read that right. The big increases in inequality in almost every Western nation happened before 1990, ahead of globalization and the digital revolution. Inconveniently for many, facts about inequality just do not fit their theories. In Britain, the Gini coefficient – that benchmark measure of income inequality – rose sharply in the decades before 1990. It has subsequently stopped rising and, if anything, has shown a slight decrease since.

In America, the top 1 per cent of income-earners still make 13 per cent less than they did in 2007 before the recession, according to Emmanuel Saez, a professor at Berkeley. The bottom 90 per cent make around 8 per cent less. The gap between rich and poor has therefore narrowed. The Congressional Budget Office's latest calculations suggest that inequality was almost 5 per cent lower in 2013, the latest year for which figures are available, than in 2007.

Nor should we accept the idea that digital means monopolies, either. It's true that at any given time, there certainly seem to be some pretty big players in the digital market place, such as Google and Facebook. But the internet is a fiercely competitive place and the barriers to entry are not unassailable. Today's giants can be displaced, just as Alta Vista and Yahoo were. The position of Facebook and Uber don't seem quite as impregnable today as they did only a couple of years ago.

If there simply isn't enough economic inequality to explain the rise of political populism, how to we account for the recent rise of this phenomenon?

DIGITAL EXPECTATIONS

Those that disapprove of the way that voters vote often imply that the electorate has been duped. In Britain, ever since the EU referendum went the 'wrong' way, some in the mainstream media have dedicated hours trying to establish some sort of conspiracy. There was, certain newspaper columnists have implied, a devilishly-clever use of data and 'fake news' involving Russians and US plutocrats or something. It's almost as if some anti-Brexit sections of the media struggle to accept that a majority of rational citizens might elect to leave the EU.

In order to come to terms with election outcomes they don't like, parts of the media categorize political populism as backward looking. Populists on the radical Left, such as Jeremy Corbyn, are all about reheated 1960s-style socialism, we are told. Those on the Right are all about a desire to return to the monocultural simplicity of the mid-twentieth century, apparently.

Does, perhaps, this kind of 'insinuate-and-insult' analysis tell us more about elite opinion-formers than it does about political populism? What if populism is not some sort of blast from the past, but a sign of things to come?

Maybe digital technology isn't about fiendish algorithms implanting a false consciousness into the minds of middle England and America. Is it simply a case of enabling dissenting voices from outside the mainstream to be heard for the first time?

Populist opinions are being heard because they now can be. A generation ago, ideas didn't get airtime unless they sat within a narrow spectrum of opinion. For a start, there were many fewer TV stations, and far less competition between them for audience share.

Who got airtime was decided by a cosy consensus between one or two established networks. Digital has created an array of TV networks and platforms, and increased the competition between them. Twenty-four-hour news channels and the creation of a news stream, rather than a news cycle, means airtime for these new voices. And if it is seen to boost ratings, they get lots of it. Thirty years ago, there were no blog sites like Breitbart or Guido Fawkes. Before 2004, there wasn't even any Twitter or Facebook.

The kind of people that ran mainstream media organizations might all agree that the issue of Britain's membership of the European Union had been sorted out long ago, or that there was no serious case to be made for a radically redistributive taxation. Millions of people on social media don't seem to agree. Arguments that once seemed settled are no longer so.

Digital has changed all sorts of public expectations. In *The Long Tail*, American author Chris Anderson foresaw how the digital marketplace would mean more choice.

Instead of having to put up with what is on offer, digital allows you to find the niche products and tastes that fit you. Instead of buying the whole album, you can download the track that you like. Rather than taking the generic brand on offer, you can find what suits you.

A generation ago, we watched what was on television whenever a TV programmer decided to schedule it. Distant DJs selected what music we listened to. Today, Netflix and Spotify allow us to programme what we want at a time that suits us.

Digital has changed people's expectations of how things could be. Self-selection has become a cultural norm. Choice and competition are expected. Perhaps rather than being a rejection of modernity, it is modernity – and the new expectations it has created – that have made the populist insurgency possible? The idea of 'taking back control' certainly seemed to resonate with the electorate during Britain's EU referendum campaign.

Digital means that there are now not just niches for opinions that are distinctive and particular. Some sections of the electorate seem so used to having their views articulated that they don't just expect to hear them, but can seem affronted at the idea of other views being given airtime – as plenty of broadcasters in Britain found out during the Scottish and Brexit referendum campaigns.

Digital has for good or ill democratized the process of forming opinion. The parameters of public policy are no longer defined by a priesthood of pundits but by the autonomous actions of millions of people. During this digital reformation, professional pundits can often be heard railing against 'fake news', like old-time priests raging against heretics. Heretics might indeed often speak a lot of nonsense but they sometimes have an annoying habit of revealing the nonsense of the priesthood, too.

POPULISM AS REBELLION

Those that feel threatened by the democratization of opinion-forming often point to the consequences of having populists in power. What they should instead do is look at populism as a consequence of who has power.

To date, some populist leaders, like Trump or Hungary's Viktor Orbán, have won the occasional election. But they have hardly established tyrannies. Donald Trump can't even seem to get his (in)famous wall built along the border with Mexico. Orbán's government has been opposed by judges, his civil servants and EU officials at every turn. In Italy and Greece, populist prime ministers are unable to decide their own budgets, having to submit them to EU officials for sign-off first.

Even when elected to office, populist leaders seem encased by bureaucracy. It's not just the separation of powers that frustrates the Trump White House. He has appeared at times to be waging a perpetual battle against the bureaucracy of the federal government itself.

Populism is in large measure a consequence of the frustration that the electorate feels against an alphabet soup of administration that is impervious to change. Across much of the Western world, the public have perceptively clocked that public policy-making is in the hands of institutions that do not answer to the public. They resent it. They realize that legislatures have become increasingly perfunctory, full of placemen, able to do little more than rubber-stamp decisions made elsewhere.

Officials are able to make laws without legislating. In Britain, something called Statutory Instruments enable ministers – or rather their officials – to change the law without going back to Parliament for permission. Government agencies issue guidelines that the courts increasingly regard as having legal force. In America, too, Congress has been deferential to federal agencies, enabling them to fill in blank canvasses handed to them by those on the Hill.

So why vote for establishment politicians that are placemen to the administrative state? Vote for colourful characters who look like they might shake things up.

ELITE CONCEIT

The philosopher Bertrand Russell once told a story about

a chicken in order to make a serious point about how some people use facts to support their favourite theories.

Each day, Russell said, a farmer came to feed this chicken corn. Based on the evidence, Russell said, if the chicken had been capable of abstract thought, it might well deduce that the farmer liked her.

When the farmer started to double the amount of corn he gave the chicken each day, the evidence for the chicken's 'friendly farmer' theory literally started to pile up. But then one day the farmer came and, instead of giving the chicken corn, he wrung her neck. Not so friendly after all.

The friendly-farmer theory might have been supported by the observable facts but it was fundamentally flawed. And the alternative 'farmer-fattening-up-chicken-to-eat' theory – also supported by the facts – might have better explained what was going on. Yet Bertrand Russell's chicken wanted to believe the farmer was friendly. It used the facts to deceive itself. So much public policy-making is similarly bird-brained.

Like that chicken, those that make public policy are so sure of themselves that they see only what they want to see. It gives rise to conceit. Not only do public administrators have an over-inflated sense of what they can achieve by design, but they ignore the evidence that ought to inform them that their ambition is unmatched by results.

Consider, for example, all those 'early intervention'

programmes in Britain designed to improve children's life chances. They never have quite the impact in terms of outcome they were supposed to. But they are a nice idea, so no one seems to want to say. No amount of evidence seems to dent the enthusiasm of social workers to try to solve problems with other people's money.

What about outreach programmes that have zero impact on reducing knife crime? How about all those prisoner rehabilitation programmes which involve staging plays, but which don't actually have any impact on reoffending rates? The reality is that the type of prisoner willing to take part in such programmes is half way to wanting to mend their ways in the first place. Selection bias, not performing Shakespeare, explains the lower recidivism, even if it sounds heartless to say so.

A common currency would in theory make Europeans richer. In practice it has reduced parts of the continent to a state of permanent penury. Central banks setting interest rates would in theory mean stability and an end to boom-and-bust. In practice, it meant they tanked the banks.

Perhaps populism is what happens when government tries to be so big and all-embracing that it inevitably underperforms?

Populism is a response to the emergence of technocracy. Alas, it is unlikely to offer any viable solutions.

———

THE PROBLEM WITH POPULISTS

In the first half of the twentieth century, Argentina was one of the richest places on the planet. An open, agricultural economy, Argentina sold farm produce to the world and imported manufactured goods from Europe and America. Her middle class prospered and many of southern Europe's poor went and settled in that land of opportunity.

Today, Argentina has fallen down the world rankings. She is somewhere between being a middle-income country and plain poor. Her government has periodically defaulted on its debts. Economic growth has often slowed and there have been whole decades when she has gone backwards. Argentina over the past sixty years has become a by-word for bad government – and serves as a warning of what can happen when populists are put in charge.

Rather than eliminate poverty as Juan Perón, Argentina's most famous populist president promised, he left the average Argentine poorer. Instead of 'dignifying workers' as the Perónist slogan demanded, his economic policies produced mass unemployment. The one part of the Perónist economic package that the government did deliver on was to make Argentina's economy independent. High tariffs did indeed isolate a country that had once been integrated with the world economy. Living standards fell.

There then followed a cycle of intermittent economic crises. Out of the episodic chaos invariably emerged other strongmen – sometimes elected, sometimes installed at the barrel of a gun. By the 1970s, the military were waging a 'dirty war', with thousands of 'the disappeared' murdered by their own government. Argentine aggression was at times projected outward, almost leading to war with Chile in the 1970s and then manifesting in the invasion of the Falkland Islands in the 1980s.

What happened to Argentina shows that populists might come to office for all sorts of understandable reasons but unless they do things that actually shift the balance back towards free exchange, they inhibit economic growth and progress as surely as any of the perceived injustices that encourage people to vote for them in the first place. Perón and co. set a successful society on a merry-go-round of redistribution and protectionism, failure and crisis.

You don't have to accept anything as outlandish as the idea that we are starting to see what you might call the Argentine-ization of European politics to worry about where populism may take us. You need not agree that there is a whiff of Perón about the current White House. Just reflect on some of the history we have been looking at. See what happened in those exceptional societies that for a time achieved progress.

In the dying days of the Roman Republic, populism

pitched the *Populares* against the *Optimates* – neither of whom stood to restore free exchange but to extort from each other instead. In Venice, Bajamonte's insurrection didn't arrest the concentration of power. It provided the oligarchy with a perfect pretext to concentrate it further still, establishing a new institution, the Council of Ten. Set up in the immediate aftermath of the failed coup, this body was to serve as the effective government of the republic for the next six hundred years.

In Holland, too, the populist leader Johanne de Witt proved so incompetent, having failed to prevent invasion, that he was murdered by an angry mob. He was no more successful than the Gracchi at taking on the elite, and ended up the same way. His main political achievement was to make the restoration of a strong sovereign – something he opposed – possible.

When have populists ever moved a society away from redistribution and protectionism towards more specialization and exchange? We should not imagine that any twenty-first-century de Witts or Peróns, Bajamontes or Gracchi would do any better.

So, what should we do to safeguard the future of free and open societies?

PART VII

WHAT IS TO
BE DONE?

22

GOVERNMENT OF
THE PEOPLE

The world is getting better. There has been the most amazing progress in the human condition over the past three hundred years – even if there have been some catastrophic reversals and plenty of late starts along the way. Despite the move towards greater technocracy within recent decades, for almost everyone around the world life is better now than ever before.

To ensure that this continues, we need to safeguard free exchange – and that means taking steps to constrain the growth of powerful elites that might otherwise hinder progress. How might this to be done?

It is not enough to try to elect the 'right' politicians. Even if those elected understand the problem, in office they end up encased in the same machinery of state as anyone else. Even the bravest ministers find themselves run by officialdom.

Nor is it enough to hope that the 'right' politicians might appoint the 'right' sort of officials to oversee the administrative state. An administrative state invariably tries to run things by official fiat, and is therefore antithetical to free exchange irrespective of whoever notionally presides over it.

Instead of seeking to control the technocratic state, we should seek to deconstruct it, denying those that preside over it the sources of their power and authority. Where decision-making has been concentrated within new bureaucratic institutions, we should seek to pass power back towards the people, with a series of far-reaching democratic reforms. Where expansive officialdom has marshalled vast resources through borrowing, we should aim to ensure that the administrative state lives once more within the tax base.

OPENING UP DEMOCRACY

To rein in those with political power, the political process needs to be made properly competitive. Politicians need to answer more directly to their electorates, and less to the party bosses, lobbyists and the various branches of the administrative state that seem so effective at setting the political agenda of those elected to high office.

Too often in many established democracies, the political process is rigged with uncompetitive practices. Stripping these out of the system would make it much harder for those in public life to lose sight of what the public thinks.

In America, for example, a system of gerrymandering has been created that allows politicians to choose their electorates, rather than the electorates choose their politicians. Each state gets an allocation of seats in the House of Representatives. What then happens is that within each state the two parties collude to carve up the state into congressional districts so that most of the districts are safe. That is to say, they become uncompetitive. Gerry-mandered seats are the twenty-first-century equivalent of a rotten borough. Congressional districts should be drawn up, as they are in the UK, on the basis of how local people define their neighbourhood, rather than how political parties would like neighbourhoods to be defined for their convenience.

It's not just in America where anti-competitive electoral practices have emerged. The UK itself has an electoral system of one MP per constituency that was only introduced in 1884 – not uncoincidentally, the same year that the working man was given the vote. What this system does is ensure that there is little competition within a constituency. Most seats in most of the General

Elections that have been held ever since stood little chance of changing hands. Naturally this suits parties, who can count on the safe return of large numbers of seats in the legislature. It's not such good news for voters who happen to live in a seat where they get taken for granted.

The effect of the UK's monopolistic electoral system was to ensure that whoever won the party nomination to be the candidate could almost always count on being elected to Parliament. This, of course, ensured that the party machine in effect got to decide who got into the legislature. Unsurprisingly, perhaps, within a few years of the introduction of the new electoral system, parties started to become more organized, with a top-down system of candidate selection and approval.

Unlike in America, where parties – relatively recently – started to open up the process for selecting candidates, little serious effort has been made to allow ordinary voters much say in the candidate selection process. A reform that would help the political process in the UK would be to introduce a system of open primary candidate selection. In America this has the effect of ensuring that even in areas that tilt heavily towards one party – or when the boundaries have been drawn to make things uncompetitive – there is at least an element of competition. New York's 14th congressional district, for example, might lean heavily towards the Democrats no matter how you draw the boundaries, but it was still possible for Alexandria

Ocasio-Cortez to defeat the incumbent Congressman in a primary contest in order to get into Congress. Irrespective of one's views of the infamously outspoken AOC, as she is known, it is surely good for democracy that new voices can compete to get into Congress.

In Europe, the electoral system seems almost designed to empower party bosses to keep out candidates and ideas that they disapprove of. Instead of having constituencies or districts, seats in many legislatures are allocated according to a party list. Each party ranks its candidates on a list. Voters then vote, determining what percentage of the seats in parliament are allocated to each party.

Unsurprisingly, parties tend to put the leadership sycophants and placemen higher up the list, and anyone that shows any form of independent thought lower down the list. That process of ranking candidates, more so than the votes of the people, tends to determine the composition of the legislature. Is it any wonder that millions of Europeans now feel that their politicians are a caste apart?

Politics on either side of the Atlantic could benefit from a general right of recall, allowing voters to sack their representatives midterm. In America, various elected officials can already be recalled in certain circumstances. However, there is no such right to recall Senators or members of Congress. The details of how recall might apply in different countries would vary but the basic principle – that the electorate can trigger a vote of confidence in their elected representative midterm – is a good one. Too many politicians serve their party interests rather than broader ones. Making them directly accountable to ordinary voters midterm would act as a necessary constraint on partisanship.

In Switzerland and some US states, voters have the power to trigger referendums. The use of referendums needs to be extended. Such is the political elite's fear of populism at present, there would be enormous opposition to the further use of plebiscites. 'Referendums aren't democratic. They are a tool for demagogues!' insist those that disapprove of the EU referendum result. Referendums are actually a pretty effective constraint against overbearing government – especially when, as in Switzerland, they are a means by which voters can veto something that the executive is seeking to do. If those that we elect are unwilling to rein in the administrative state, the electorate should be given the right to do so directly.

Removing various anti-competitive practices from the political process, and introducing a right of recall, more referendums and open primary contests, might help ensure more competition in the political process. But would it ensure that the new, competitive politics was any more inclined to rein in the administrative state?

If we are serious about checking it, we need to restore the most fundamental constraint on big government: the link between taxation and representation.

REPRESENTATION AND
TAXATION

For as long as any extra government spending meant higher taxes, the taxpayer could be counted on to vote in a way that would keep government small. Richard Nixon's decision to make the US dollar a fiat currency in 1971 broke the link between taxation and representation. It's worth delving a little deeper to understand how and why a change in the way that we managed money had such an impact on democracy.

Once the dollar was converted into a paper currency, no longer backed by gold, the government could do two things on an unprecedented scale; borrow money and debase its value. Both enable officialdom to live beyond the tax base.

If a dollar issued is no longer backed by a quantity of gold, there is no longer this basic constraint on the number of dollars put into circulation. Government can in effect print more and more money, diminishing the value of that in circulation. This inflation is a form of taxation, since it transfers wealth from those that use or hold the currency (the value of what they have goes down) to the state that issued the extra money in the first place.

To put into perspective the inflation that has happened since 1971, reflect on what happened in Rome between

317

AD 1 and 200. Over the course of two centuries, successive Roman emperors cut the silver content of the *denarius* by about 90 per cent. What it took the Romans two centuries to do, our governments have achieved in two generations. Since 1971, inflation has diminished the value of the US dollar and pound sterling by about the same amount.

But it's not just inflation that the shift towards a paper currency allowed. What happened in 1971 has enabled government to borrow enormous amounts, too. Since the seventeenth century, if not earlier, when a government has needed to spend more money than it takes in tax, it has issued a bond, an IOU. A bank, or in early modern times an especially rich family, might have lent a government or ruler cash up front in return for a bond that promised to pay them back a certain amount over time, out of future taxation.

Unlike setting tax rates, neither the House of Commons nor Congress has ever had control over how many bonds the Treasury issues. But what limited the ability of government to borrow from the bond market was, to put it crudely, the willingness of banks to lend. Making the US dollar a fiat currency suddenly enabled banks to create vastly more credit than had been possible before. The willingness of banks to buy bonds increased dramatically from the early 1970s. Indeed, billion-dollar bond markets sprang up around the Western world on a scale that was without precedent. Buying up all this government debt on behalf of all kinds of investors became big business.

Suddenly it became extremely easy for a government, faced with less tax revenue than they might like, to increase what it was prepared to offer at its regular bond auction. No one need vote to raise taxes. There would be no harmful electoral response from voters angry that they were having to pay for all the things they had been told they had a right to expect. Deficits and debt rose. Bond dealers made fortunes. And the administrative state was able to expand.

Like some of those oil-rich autocrats who don't depend on the permission of their people for what they are able to spend, public administration has grown more lavish and less responsive. Of course, if you are a dictator in an oil-rich country, you don't depend on having to appease the electorate to hold office. But even so, if you have any sense, you will from time to time use some of the wealth that you have to bribe the masses. Western governments do have to think far more about how to keep their electorates on side, so the incentive to bribe voters with the proceeds of the bond market is never far away.

Imagine the effect of forcing the state to spend only what it was prepared to take in tax? In America, government spending is currently about 37 per cent of GDP, yet the tax take is only about 26 per cent of GDP. The difference is the annual deficit.

If what the state spent was the same as what it took in tax, either there would have to be an almighty increase in taxation – followed by a massive anti-tax backlash – or vast swathes of the administrative state would have to be shut down permanently.

This is the only really effective way to deconstruct the technocratic state. Electing conservative-sounding politicians has done little to help. But ensuring that government can no longer live beyond its tax base requires changing the way we manage money.

CHANGING THE WAY WE MANAGE MONEY

The Watergate scandal might now be a mere memory, but the consequences of Richard Nixon's decision to turn the dollar into a fiat currency are still with us; expansive officialdom has been given free rein to fund vast budget deficits. What should we do about this? Although at some point in the future, China – which has built up very large gold reserves – could establish a link between its currency and the value of gold, it's difficult to see a return to any kind of gold standard as a solution.

Apart from anything else, decreeing that the US dollar or Chinese Renminbi is worth a certain amount of precious metal is a form of price-fixing. As Britain discovered when we returned to gold after the First World War, fixing the price of anything arbitrarily can have all sorts of unintended consequences.

We do not need a grand scheme to fix the world currency system. We need a system that allows the currency system to evolve of its own accord. The original nineteenth-century gold standard evolved in precisely such a way. It was not the product of any top-down design.

How might one allow a currency system to develop that did not simply serve the interests of technocratic states, intent on spending what they weren't prepared to ask their electorates to pay in taxation?

Firstly, we need to limit the ability of banks to conjure vast quantities of credit out of thin air. Unless and until we do so, governments will have almost unlimited takers for its IOUs, and so be able to spend with few limits. Quite apart from all the harm that credit bubbles cause – inflating asset prices, producing malinvestment and ending in inevitable busts – it is fundamentally what has fuelled the growth of big government.

A bank's ability to conjure credit out of nothing is based on a simple point of law. If you deposit money into your bank account, you no longer own that money. The bank does. You merely hold a legal claim to it. Since the bank now legally owns what you paid into it, it is legally able to lend against it – often multiple times. This system of fractional reserve banking has been around a long time. But before money became just a paper promise, fractional reserve banking could not produce quite the quantities of credit we see today. The fiat money, when mixed with unrestrained fractional reserve banking, enables almost limitless credit creation.

This is precisely why, in the aftermath of the Nixon shock of 1971, credit controls – limiting what banks could do with their unrestrained credit-creating powers – were needed. It was once those proved ineffective that we moved towards monetarism – a policy of trying to control the money supply not with credit controls but by manipulation of interest rates. One could almost argue that the history of monetary policy in the advanced industrial nations since 1971 has been a series of failed attempts to deal with the unintended consequences of giving banks the power of unlimited credit-creation.

What if we limited the credit that banks could conjure up by changing the law so that, unless the customers explicitly agreed otherwise, the money that they deposited with a bank was legally theirs, not the banks?* Banks might then have two tiers of bank accounts – ones in which the customer retained ownership (deposit accounts) and those where the bank was free to lend out multiple times (lending accounts). If that happened,

---

* I presented a bill in the House of Commons to achieve this legal change in November 2010 as the Financial Services (Regulation of Deposits and Lending) Bill.

presumably the interest rates would be lower in the former kind of accounts, and higher in those accounts where the bank was able to lend against the deposit and earn an income.

The total amount of money that customers place in a bank's deposit accounts relative to the money that they leave in the bank's lending accounts would become, in effect, the bank's reserve ratio. If customers trusted a bank, the ratio of money they left in lending accounts would rise, relative to that in deposit accounts. In other words, the reserve ratio would rise. Conversely, if customers didn't trust those managing their bank, the reserve ratio of the bank would fall.

As well as creating a banking system that made it harder for officialdom to engage in a symbiotic relationship with big banks in order to live beyond their means, such a series of reforms might also provide a free-market way of managing financial risk, guarding us against excessive leverage of the kind that has on several occasions threatened to damage the global economic system.

'But these sorts of changes would ruin our economic system as we know it!' some will say. 'We need the credit to grow!' Actually, in 2007 the current banking system did a pretty good job of crashing the world economy – and changing the law so that banks could no longer automatically lend against a customer's deposits would not end credit. It would not even end fractional reserve banking. It might just help ensure that credit tended to correlate more closely with someone's saving – and deferred consumption. Capital would be allocated on the basis of actual economic demand, rather than official-dom's appetite for debt. And officialdom would have to learn to live with fewer deficits and less debt.

INSTEAD OF SUPRANATIONALISM

It is thanks to democratic innovation – in this case, the use of a referendum – that Britain is able to leave the European Union. It took a plebiscite to enable Britain to break free from a technocratic state that is stifling inno-vation and growth. Hopefully, the use of more direct democracy will enable other European states to break free from a failing Union.

But how might we manage international relations instead? If everyone left the EU, is there not a danger that Europe would return to a mosaic of nation states, imposing all sorts of restrictions on each other?

That is certainly what the political elite in Brussels would say. Without an army of officials, trade barriers would go up – and living standards would come down. If there was less trade, we would certainly be worse off. But why would having fewer rule-makers making all those rules mean more protectionist trade policies? On the contrary, aren't they the cause of the permission-based regulations in the first place?

The real alternative is to have a system of free trade, achieved through mutual standard-recognition. Imagine that you go on holiday to America. You eat food that has been approved by US regulators. You might drive a car that has met US federal standards. Fancy a bit of shopping at the local mall? You will buy clothes that have been manufactured to a US specification. If, heaven forbid, you fell ill, you would be treated with medicines that had been approved by the federal pharmaceutical regulator, the FDA.

You would not refuse any of those products because they had been approved by a US, rather than a UK or EU, regulator. So why is it that when you return to the UK, you are prevented from consuming any of those items unless they have also been approved by a UK or EU regulator? If we had real free trade, you wouldn't be. A free-trade agreement between several countries would mean that whatever it was legal to buy and sell in one could be legally bought and sold in the others, too. Each country would continue to go about regulating its own affairs. But if citizens wanted to buy something that had been approved for use by another country's regulator, they would be free to do so. Rather than one uniform set of standards, there would be multiple.

Multiple standards are not so unusual; indeed, they are already the norm in education. Today in Britain, sixth-formers sit an exam when they are eighteen. In many cases the exam is an A-level. But some can sit the International Baccalaureate instead. Some sit AS-levels, too. Others do none of those things but sit something called a Pre-U exam instead. Each of those exams is, in their different way, an assessment of what the pupil has learnt.

Mutual standard-recognition between comparable Western regulatory regimes would produce something similar. Just as someone is free to sit the International Baccalaureate exams administered by a body in Switzerland, so we would be free to buy chocolate or cheese approved by a Swiss regulator. Indeed, restricting that freedom makes very little sense. The government does not ban you from buying and bringing back home US-regulated products if you visit the States. So why do they presume to ban you from buying them once you're back in the UK?

'Might this not mean a regulatory race to the bottom?' No. Regulators would still have a legal duty to keep people safe but you might get a regulatory regime that was a little more circumspect and considered. If the UK regulator knew that another rule-maker was having to make the same assessments that they were having to make, it would be more careful to ensure that the rules they imposed were proportionate. The onus would be on regulating what needed regulating, rather than making rules as an end in itself.

Regulators might stick to regulating the outcomes – the functionality of the finished product – rather than interfering as they increasingly do with the process of its production. Moreover, because more than one agency would determine the standards in any one area, the system would be less open to lobbying by vested interests looking to rig the rules to their advantage. If one regulatory agency was captured by a particular vested interest – as many have been – they could not skew the market a certain way as easily as they do so today.

'Might not a system of different regulatory regimes lead to chaos and complexity?' Quite the opposite. It's the current attempts to impose uniform standards in the European Single Market, and to govern transatlantic trade through TTIP, that create complexity and confusion – not to mention a blizzard of red tape. Trying to harmonize different standards will always be more complicated than permitting both.

Mutual standard-recognition will allow us to have regulation without constricting the consumer; it would reconcile independence – nations making their own rules – with interdependence – the need to allow individual buyers and sellers to exchange freely. Specialization and exchange, which is what drives human progress, would be secure.

INSTITUTIONAL CHANGE
IS NOT ENOUGH

Imagine if back in the first century AD you had wanted to try to restore the old Roman Republican system of government. What would have been your first step? One measure might be to abolish some of the new imperial institutions, such as Augustus' new *Consilium Principis*, and return the powers they exercised back to the Senate, or even to elected magistrates.

Or what if you lived in fourteenth-century Venice, and you wanted to ensure that power within the republic was dispersed more widely once again? It would have made sense perhaps to have proposed abolishing the Council of Ten, and handed its executive responsibilities to a larger, more broadly representative body.

One only has to think of institutional change in these terms to appreciate that institutional reform is not enough. Just as the shape of a society's institutions cannot of itself account for why power is dispersed, neither can power be dispersed within a society through institutional change alone.

Abolishing part of Augustus' imperial bureaucracy would not have restored the Roman Republic. A bit of additional institutional tinkering to an already inordinately complex Venetian constitution would not have opened up the oligarchy. Neither is institutional change today going to be enough to keep power dispersed and free exchange secure.

What about the idea that we might rein in the system of 'imperial' technocracy that has emerged in Europe and America by cutting it off from more money? If government on either side of the Atlantic had to live within its tax base, would that be enough to ensure limited government? It would certainly help if officialdom could no longer borrow on such a vast scale.

Yet we know from what has happened each time that the US Congress has withheld funding from the federal government what sort of backlash ensues. Congress comes under enormous political pressure – irrespective of who sits in the Oval office – to be generous with the tax dollars that a future generation of Americans has not even paid yet.

If we want to ensure that power in free societies remains dispersed, we need to tackle the impulse for greater intervention in social and economic affairs itself. We need to change some of the underlying assumptions society has about the rights and wrongs of free exchange in the first place.

23

THE CASE FOR
FREE EXCHANGE

No matter how complex a country's constitution or sophisticated the institutional constraints imposed upon its rulers, none of it will prevent the concentration of power if ordering society from on high is thought to be the right thing to do. Nothing makes the idea of top-down design appear more desirable – indeed essential – than pessimism.

PROGRESS Vs. PESSIMISM

The story of human progress is remarkable and uplifting – yet it's seldom told. One of the reasons is that pessimism – the notion that progress has not happened and that left to themselves things will get worse – provides a very powerful pretext for those intent upon intervening in the affairs of others. Why? Because if you believe that the world is getting worse, you invite the idea that there needs to be some sort of intervention to put things right.

From Jacobins to Marxists to today's radical environmentalists, those intent on ordering society according to some sort of scheme always start out by insisting that the world has been getting worse.

Rousseau suggested that the human condition had somehow descended from a pristine past. It was on the back of this pessimistic view of human history that the Jacobins established a dictatorship that tried to make society from scratch. Marx argued that history was a grim story of class struggle. Today, many 'progressives' reject the notion that there has been much human progress at all. Even if the human condition has improved, they insist, progress has happened only as a result of catastrophic environmental degradation, or the exploitation of women or minorities by a patriarchy.

Pessimism served as a pretext in pre-modern times, too. Which is why it pervades the creation myths of those patrimonial societies of the past. In the Aztec creation myth, Huitzilopochtli kicks things off by murdering most members of his family. In Egypt, Ra gave rise to humans when he wept and bled. In ancient Chinese mythology, people came into existence as the fleas from Pangu's corpse. In the old testament, Adam and Eve fell from grace and were expelled from Eden. None of it is cheerful stuff, is it? And it is doom and gloom for a purpose.

Those at the apex of society intent on ordering it to their own advantage have always had to promote a pessimistic world view. The sun god might not arise anew each morning. The rains might fail. The souls of sinners might remain in perpetual purgatory. Without the intervention of experts, social inequality might increase or the climate will collapse or the oceans turn to acid. Or AI will take our jobs and automation will mean mass unemployment. Or Europe will see a re-run of world war. Or something.

Unless, of course, we accept the need for whatever grandiose intervention it is we are told will save the situation. So pay the tithe, tolls and taxes, submit to the wisdom of priests and experts. Allow the elites to shape public policy as they insist – and all will be well. Submit to the authority of some supranational agency, and we can avert such apocalyptic disasters. Just like in pre-modern times, we are asked to believe that giving other people authority over us will somehow restore the world to a kind of equilibrium.

But what if the world manages just fine by itself? What if things are actually looking up, and don't really need any sort of top-down direction? What if people all came to appreciate that it is not just the sun and the rains, or the souls of sinners, but social equality and opportunity and material improvements that are able to take care of themselves?

Then there would be much less need to place at centre stage those that insist that they might order our affairs. This is why telling the story of our elevation is so subversive – and so necessary.

Pessimism isn't just a question of downplaying human progress. It is also about implying that progress, even when it happens, is somehow incidental. That it is down to something other than human agency and ingenuity.

We are repeatedly invited to believe that the reason why some societies have advanced further than others is a matter of luck or geography or the local ecology. Or it's because of the prevalence of guns, germs and steel. Or the ease with which local fauna and flora could be domesticated. Anything, it seems, to avoid the conclusion that some societies might have done better than others because of the way that they arrange themselves.

Hobbes' seventeenth-century heresy was to suggest that an improvement in the human condition could be accounted for by the effect of a strong sovereign. The heresy today is to suggest that it is free markets that explain human progress.

Jared Diamond, the best-selling historian whose ideas about the past have influenced millions of people, finds all sorts of ecological factors to account for why some societies flourished relative to others in the past.

Looking forward, he warns of catastrophic environmental depletion ahead. Collapse can only be averted, apparently, by adopting some sort of blueprint. Making human agency incidental to the story of human progress turns out to be intrinsically pessimistic, and makes it easier to justify ordering society from above by fiat and force.

Once we appreciate that there has been progress, we are no longer beholden to the sense that we need to submit our society to orders from above in order that it might be 'saved'. It's not class struggle, or the exploitation of other people or the environment that account for our increase in living standards, but our own agency and ingenuity.

Undirected human agency is not just the engine of progress. The idea that it might be is an affront to any sense that society should be organised by others; which is precisely why so much effort goes into finding all kinds of external factors – extraneous, rather than human agency, you might almost say – to account for human progress instead.

It's not only pessimism that is used to undermine the idea of a free society. So, too, is the notion that there is something immoral about free exchange. Free exchange is in reality morally superior to any other form of exchange – and the best way to illustrate this is perhaps to start with a cup of coffee.

FREE Vs. FORCED EXCHANGE

Moments before I typed this sentence, I spent £3 on a cappuccino here in my favourite London café. It might sound obvious, but I bought a cup of coffee because I wanted it more than I wanted the £3 I used to pay for it. And conversely the café owner sold me the coffee because he preferred to have £3 rather than the coffee that he served me. So we swapped, and were both better off as a result.

This simple idea extends all the way along the various processes that go into producing a cappuccino. The person that worked the coffee machine, the farmer whose herd of cows produced the milk, the company that made the cup I drank from, and – of course – the farmer that grew the coffee beans; each one of them was prompted to sell some of what it was that went into making my cup of coffee because they stood to gain from the exchange.

'But what about the poor farmer in Africa, who only got a small fraction of the £3 you paid? Surely its exploitative that the person that produced such a key ingredient only got a small amount of the money?' some will say.

Alongside pessimism, this idea that the exchange is exploitative is another pernicious idea used to justify ordering human affairs by design. The implication is that we cannot have some sort of spontaneous economic order without someone somewhere being worse off as a result.

But this kind of claim that free exchange is exploitative is simply not true.

Why would either the coffee farmer or anyone else in the production process freely sell their produce unless they were better off after the transaction than they were before? To be sure, the coffee farmer – much like everyone else that contributed to the supply process to produce the coffee – might have preferred it if they were paid more, but by definition they would not have entered into the exchange freely unless it left them better off than before.

If you believe that the coffee farmer who grew the beans that made my coffee was underpaid for his produce, why stop with him? What about the barista that worked the coffee machine? Or the dairy farmer who puts in such long and lonely hours with their herd? Why not pay them more, too, on the basis of what we feel to be fair? That would be better, right? Wrong.

If we paid people on the basis of some sort of arbitrary assessment of what it felt right to pay them, my coffee would have probably cost me not £3, but £5 or more. And at that point, I would prefer to keep the money in my bank, and not swap it for a cup of coffee at all.

So there would be less custom, and everyone that stood to gain from my purchase of a £3 cup of coffee would be worse off.

This is precisely what happens, on a far greater scale, when we allow arbitrary ideas of worth and value to determine what people pay for what others produce. It's why countries that try to pay people on the basis of what others feel to be fair – like Uganda in the 1970s or Venezuela today – end up with chronic shortages and poverty. A product – a cup of coffee or any other – is not worth what we 'feel' it ought to be worth, but what people are actually prepared to do for it.

This is what makes free exchange morally superior to any other system of exchange.

None of this is to say that there are not circumstances in which it might be necessary and morally justifiable to find other ways to allocate resources. It would be right in certain circumstances, for example, to commandeer someone else's property to save a life. There are times when it is legitimate for the state to commandeer things from citizens in defence of some overarching interest: it's right that we do jury service in the interest of justice; or in national emergencies for the military service to defend the nation; or to pay taxes in the interest of helping the helpless. But exchange undertaken freely is always morally *preferable* to any other basis for exchange.

Free exchange is morally preferable to forced exchange, yet we are constantly asked to believe the opposite – that the division of labour is at best undignified, and at worst exploitative. According to the French economist Thomas Piketty, Western economies are programmed to fail. Returns on capital, he argued in his best-selling book, accumulate inexorably faster than the economy grows. This, Piketty suggests, will lead to a concentration of wealth, giving rise to unsustainable inequality and unrest.*

Pessimism and inequality for Piketty necessitate redistribution. What might just save the day, however, is if we put our faith in economists like him, who are able to understand the problem and devise a system of redistribution that will restore everything to equilibrium. Marxists, of course, have spent more than a century making much the same point. Any sort of spontaneous economic order, they insist, ends in exploitation and class war. Free exchange cannot improve the human condition; only a state taking from one class and giving to another can create order and progress, they say.

Such ideas about redistribution have recently been given a new lease of life with calls for a UBI, or Universal Basic Income.

NEW Vs. OLD IDEAS
ABOUT REDISTRIBUTION

No tech conference these days seems complete without at least one of its participants emoting about the effect

---

* See Piketty T., *Capital in the Twenty First Century* (2013).

of automation. This will create mass unemployment, they say, and the only answer will be for the state to pay every citizen a regular sum of money, unconditionally, out of government funds. This, apparently, can be paid for by taxing a few tech zillionaires, the very success of whose companies necessitates such payments in the first place.

The trouble is that there's very little actual evidence that paying people a Universal Basic Income is either necessary or works. It's simply false to suggest that automation has created widespread unemployment. Machines have been taking jobs done by humans for over two hundred years, yet far from causing mass hardship, there have never been more jobs in most Western states than there are today.

In Finland, where a pilot UBI programme has been run, results showed no evidence whatsoever that paying people a UBI achieved much in terms of helping unemployed people back into work.* Those that had jobs at the start of the project tended to be in work at the end of it. Those that were not gainfully employed before they received a regular payment, tended not to be in work despite receiving it.

If the purpose of the UBI is to help those whose livelihoods have been impacted by digital disruption, might

---

* See the basic income experiment 2017–2018 in Finland, (2019) preliminary results published by the Finnish Ministry of Social Affairs and Health.

it not make more sense to help such people specifically, rather than offer payments to everyone?

And in a world were digital enables much more personalization, with individualised playlists and banking services, does it make sense to adopt a blanket system of welfare provision, which takes no account of personal circumstances? Surely a truly modern system of welfare would be one that personalized payments, making full use of technology to track both taxes paid in, family circumstances and the number of dependents and needs?

It's not even as if the idea of a Universal Basic Income is actually new, for goodness sake. Something rather like it was introduced in Rome back in 123 BC, when Tiberius Gracchus created the corn dole.

Then, like now, there was apparently a problem of mass unemployment – or at least that is what advocates for the system said. It was not any sort of automation that put Roman citizens out of work, but the mass importation of slave labour – or so Tiberius Gracchus suggested. All those slaves put to work on the giant farming estates were denying honest Roman citizens the ability to earn an income, apparently. So along came Gracchus to offer every Roman citizen the right to claim a basic allowance of subsidized – soon, free – corn.

The corn dole wasn't about altruism, but was a system of imperial extortion. It wasn't about tackling the inequalities of the age – vast and growing though they were. It was a way for the Roman elite to give the plebs a share of the plunder that they were extracting from the provinces. Like wealth redistribution today, it entrenched inequality, cementing the Roman plebs in their position of dependency – and putting great power in the hands of whoever was able to control the flow of free corn into Rome from far flung provinces.

In every age, when wealth is allocated by redistribution, rather than by the autonomous actions of the market, those with political power are able to amass a great deal of it. This is why elites often rather like the idea of redistributing wealth. When you accumulate wealth through a system of fixes and favours, it's not the wealth that you amass that gets redistributed.

SELF-ORDER IS BETTER THAN DESIGN

Of course, many of those that advocate UBI are heroically indifferent to the evidence that it doesn't work. No kind of counter argument can persuade them. Like those that insist that the world is getting worse, or those who are adamant that free exchange is inherently exploitative, their argument is really about something else.

'The urge to save humanity' once wrote the American author HL Mencken, 'is almost always a false-front for the urge to rule it'. Those today who claim that they crave greater equality for society often really want to shape it. Those who insist that progress is not possible unless we implement their plan seem most intent on being the implementers.

We might defend ourselves against the ambition of those who seek to hold power over us with all manner of legal safeguards, but it is only by exposing the fraudulence of these claims of moral superiority that we can be secure.

Self-ordering societies are under attack by both conservatives and progressives, each of whom would rather use the apparatus of the state to impose their blueprint on the rest of us. Self-order is their common enemy – and the surest way to defend it is to make the moral case for self-order. In doing so we must seek to delegitimise the claims on those who make claims upon the rest of us.

Societies that are open to free exchange are not only materially and technologically better off. Self-ordering societies often prove to be morally better places, with more equality, hope and opportunity for everyone, too.

INDEX